Illinois Real Estate

Illinois Real Estate License Exam: Best Test Prep Book to Help You Get Your License!

The Ultimate Workbook: Salesperson and Broker Exam-Passing Strategies

By: Blueocean Experts
Table of Content

Introduction

Welcome to "Illinois Real Estate Learning: Best Test Prep Book to Help You Get Your License!"
If you're reading this, it means you're taking the first step toward a rewarding career in real estate
in the state of Illinois. This book is designed to be your comprehensive guide, covering everything
you need to know to pass the Illinois Real Estate License Exam and embark on a successful
career.

Why Illinois?

Illinois is a state of diverse opportunities when it comes to real estate. From the bustling
metropolis of Chicago to the serene landscapes of Southern Illinois, the state offers a range of
property types and markets that can suit any real estate professional's career goals. Whether you're
interested in residential, commercial, or industrial real estate, Illinois has something for everyone.
This book will prepare you for the unique challenges and opportunities that come with practicing
real estate in Illinois.

What's Inside?

This book is divided into several chapters, each focusing on a different aspect of real estate as
practiced in Illinois. We'll start with an overview of the Illinois real estate market, followed by a
deep dive into the eligibility criteria and application process for obtaining your license. You'll also
find chapters on property valuation, legal considerations, ethics, and much more. Each chapter is
designed to give you a thorough understanding of the subject matter, complete with examples,
tips, and practice questions.

Mock Exams

One of the most valuable resources in this book is the set of mock exams included after each chapter. These questions are designed to mimic the format and difficulty level of the actual Illinois Real Estate License Exam. Each mock exam comes with detailed explanations for each answer, helping you understand not just the "what," but also the "why" behind each question. This will enable you to identify your strengths and weaknesses and focus your study efforts accordingly.

Real-World Insights

In addition to the academic material, this book also offers real-world insights from experienced Illinois real estate professionals. These insights will give you a glimpse into the day-to-day life of a real estate agent or broker, helping you understand what to expect once you've obtained your license.

Your Journey Starts Here

Becoming a licensed real estate professional in Illinois is not just about passing an exam; it's about building a career that can offer both financial rewards and personal satisfaction. This book aims to be your go-to resource for both the exam and the early days of your career, offering you the knowledge and confidence you need to succeed.

Understanding the Illinois Real Estate Market

The Illinois real estate market is as diverse as the state itself, offering a wide range of opportunities for both buyers and sellers. From the skyscrapers of Chicago to the farmlands of central Illinois, the state's real estate landscape is a mix of urban and rural, modern and historical. This chapter aims to provide an in-depth understanding of the Illinois real estate market, covering key areas such as market trends, property types, and regional variations.

- Market Overview

Economic Factors

Illinois is the fifth most populous state in the U.S., with a GDP that ranks it among the top 20 economies in the world. The state is a hub for various industries, including manufacturing, agriculture, and technology. These economic factors play a significant role in driving the real estate market. High employment rates and a strong economy generally lead to increased demand for both residential and commercial properties.

Property Types

The Illinois real estate market is diverse, offering a range of property types:

Residential: Single-family homes, multi-family units, condos, and townhouses.
Commercial: Office buildings, retail spaces, and industrial properties.
Agricultural: Farmlands and ranches.
Specialty: Hotels, hospitals, and educational institutions.

- Regional Variations

Chicago and Surrounding Areas

Chicago, the largest city in Illinois, has a real estate market that is a microcosm of the larger state but with its unique characteristics. The city offers a range of property types, from high-rise condos to historic brownstones. The suburbs, such as Naperville and Evanston, offer more residential options, often with larger plots of land.

Central Illinois

This region is characterized by smaller cities like Springfield and Peoria and is known for its agricultural lands. The real estate market here is generally more affordable but offers fewer high-value properties like those found in Chicago.

Southern Illinois

Known for its natural beauty, Southern Illinois offers a range of recreational and vacation properties. The Shawnee National Forest is a significant attraction, and properties near this area can command higher prices.

- Market Trends

Urbanization

The trend of urbanization is strong in Illinois, especially in and around Chicago. This has led to increased demand for apartments and condos.

Sustainability

Green buildings and sustainable architecture are becoming increasingly popular. Properties that adhere to sustainability standards often command higher prices.

Technology

The integration of smart home technology is a growing trend in Illinois, particularly in new constructions. Features like smart thermostats and advanced security systems are becoming standard.

Investment Opportunities

Rental Properties

With a large student population and a steady influx of professionals, rental properties are a good investment. Cities like Urbana-Champaign, home to the University of Illinois, offer excellent opportunities for rental income.

Commercial Real Estate

Given Illinois' strong economy, investing in commercial properties like office spaces or retail units can provide good returns.

Flipping Properties

The diverse range of properties in Illinois offers numerous opportunities for property flipping, especially in up-and-coming neighborhoods.

- Challenges and Risks

Property Taxes

Illinois has some of the highest property taxes in the U.S., which can impact both buying and selling decisions.

Market Volatility

Like any real estate market, Illinois is subject to economic fluctuations. It's crucial to understand the market conditions before making an investment.

- Conclusion

Understanding the Illinois real estate market requires a multi-faceted approach, considering economic indicators, property types, regional variations, and current trends. Whether you're looking to buy, sell, or invest, a deep understanding of the market will be your most valuable asset.

Eligibility Criteria

Becoming a licensed real estate professional in Illinois is a multi-step process that requires meeting specific eligibility criteria. This chapter aims to provide a comprehensive guide to understanding these criteria, from educational requirements to background checks and everything in between.

Educational Requirements

Pre-License Education

Before you can even apply for the real estate exam, you must complete a pre-license education course. In Illinois, this consists of 75 hours of coursework from an accredited institution.

Course Components

Real Estate Principles and Practices: 60 hours
Illinois Real Estate Law: 15 hours

Continuing Education

After obtaining your license, you'll need to complete 12 hours of continuing education every two years to keep your license active.

- Age and Residency Requirements

Age

You must be at least 18 years old to apply for a real estate license in Illinois.

Residency

While Illinois does not require you to be a resident to apply for a license, you must have a sponsoring broker who is licensed in Illinois.

- Background Check and Fingerprinting

Criminal History

Illinois requires all applicants to undergo a criminal background check. While a criminal record does not automatically disqualify you, it may be reviewed by the Illinois Department of Financial and Professional Regulation (IDFPR).

Fingerprinting

Fingerprinting is a mandatory part of the background check and must be done through an approved vendor.

- Financial Responsibility

Credit Report

Some states require a credit report to assess your financial responsibility. While Illinois doesn't mandate this, a poor credit history could potentially impact your ability to work with certain brokerage firms.

- Application Process

Application Form

The application form requires detailed information, including your educational background, employment history, and any criminal records.

Fees

The application fee for a real estate license in Illinois is around $125, though this can vary. This fee is non-refundable.

Sponsoring Broker

Before your license can be issued, you must have a sponsoring broker. This is a licensed real estate broker who will supervise your activities.

- Examination Requirements

Exam Eligibility

Only after meeting the educational and background check requirements can you apply for the Illinois Real Estate Examination.

Exam Components

The exam consists of two parts:

National Portion: Covers general real estate principles.
State-Specific Portion: Focuses on Illinois real estate laws and practices.

Passing Score

You must achieve a score of at least 75% on both portions of the exam to pass.

- Special Cases: Reciprocity and License Reinstatement

Reciprocity

Illinois has reciprocity agreements with several states. If you're already licensed in one of these states, you may be able to bypass some of the educational requirements.

License Reinstatement

If your license has been inactive or expired for more than two years, you'll need to retake the pre-license education and the state exam.

- Ethical and Professional Standards

Code of Ethics

All licensed real estate professionals in Illinois are expected to adhere to a strict code of ethics, which is enforced by the IDFPR.

Disciplinary Actions

Failure to meet these ethical standards can result in disciplinary actions, ranging from fines to license revocation.

- Conclusion

Meeting the eligibility criteria for obtaining a real estate license in Illinois is a rigorous but rewarding process. From educational qualifications to background checks and ethical standards, each requirement serves to ensure that only the most qualified individuals are entrusted with the responsibilities that come with being a real estate professional in Illinois.

By understanding and fulfilling these criteria, you're not just taking steps to launch a new career; you're also ensuring that you're well-prepared for the challenges and opportunities that lie ahead in the dynamic field of real estate.

Application Process

The application process for obtaining a real estate license in Illinois is a multi-faceted journey that requires meticulous attention to detail. This chapter aims to guide you through each step, from initial preparations to the final submission of your application.

- Pre-Application Preparations

Educational Requirements

Before you begin the application process, ensure that you have completed the required 75 hours of pre-license education from an accredited institution. Keep all certificates and transcripts handy, as you will need to submit them.

Background Check and Fingerprinting

Complete your background check and fingerprinting through an approved vendor. This is crucial for the application process.

Sponsoring Broker

Secure a sponsoring broker who will supervise your activities once you are licensed. This broker must be licensed in Illinois.

- The Application Form

Where to Obtain

The application form can be downloaded from the Illinois Department of Financial and Professional Regulation (IDFPR) website or obtained from your pre-license education provider.

Sections of the Application Form

Personal Information: Includes your full name, address, and social security number.
Educational Background: Details of your pre-license education.
Employment History: Last five years of employment.
Criminal History: Any criminal records must be disclosed.
Sponsoring Broker Information: Details of your sponsoring broker.

Required Documents

Proof of Age: Usually, a copy of your driver's license or passport.
Educational Certificates: Proof of completing the pre-license education.
Background Check Results: Must be submitted along with the application.
Fingerprint Receipt: Proof of fingerprinting.

Application Fees

The application fee is around $125 and is non-refundable. Payment methods vary but usually include check, money order, or online payment.

- Submission of Application

Online Submission

The IDFPR allows for online submission of applications, which is the fastest method. You'll need to create an account on their website to proceed.

Mail Submission

You can also mail your application along with all required documents and fees to the IDFPR. This method is slower and requires careful packaging to ensure that all documents reach safely.

In-Person Submission

Some applicants prefer to submit their applications in person. This can be done at the IDFPR office during business hours.

- Application Review and Approval

Timeline

The IDFPR usually takes 4-6 weeks to review applications. This can vary based on the volume of applications they are handling.

Status Tracking

You can track the status of your application online through the IDFPR website.

Approval Notification

Once your application is approved, you will receive a notification, and your license will be issued. If there are any issues, the IDFPR will contact you for clarification or additional documentation.

- Common Mistakes to Avoid

Incomplete Forms: Ensure all sections are filled out.
Missing Documents: Double-check that all required documents are included.
Incorrect Fees: Make sure to send the correct amount.

Failure to Disclose Information: Always be honest and complete in your disclosures.

- Special Cases

Reciprocity Applications

If you are already licensed in a state with which Illinois has a reciprocity agreement, you may be eligible for an expedited application process. However, you will still need to submit an application and meet Illinois-specific requirements.

License Reinstatement

If you are applying to reinstate an expired license, additional forms and fees will be required. You may also need to retake the pre-license education and state exam.

- Conclusion

The application process for a real estate license in Illinois is a thorough and detailed procedure designed to ensure that only qualified individuals enter the profession. By following this guide, you can navigate the complexities of the application process and take a significant step toward a successful career in real estate.

By understanding the intricacies of the application process, you're not just fulfilling a bureaucratic requirement; you're also laying the foundation for a successful and ethical career in one of the most dynamic industries in Illinois.

Exam Format

The Illinois Real Estate License Exam is a critical milestone on your path to becoming a licensed real estate professional in the state of Illinois. This chapter aims to provide you with a comprehensive understanding of the exam format, types of questions you'll encounter, and strategies to maximize your chances of passing.

- Overview of the Exam

Exam Provider

The Illinois Real Estate License Exam is administered by PSI Exams, a testing service that specializes in licensing and certification exams.

Exam Sections

The exam is divided into two main sections:

National Portion: Covers general real estate principles and practices that apply across the United States.
State-Specific Portion: Focuses on laws, regulations, and practices unique to Illinois.

Number of Questions

The exam consists of 140 multiple-choice questions:

- *National Portion: 100 questions*
- *State-Specific Portion: 40 questions*

Time Limit

You will have a total of 4 hours to complete the exam:

- *National Portion: 2.5 hours*
- *State-Specific Portion: 1.5 hours*

Passing Score

The passing score for each section is as follows:

- *National Portion: 75%*
- *State-Specific Portion: 75%*

- Types of Questions

Recall

These questions test your ability to recall facts and figures. For example, "What is the minimum age requirement for obtaining a real estate license in Illinois?"

Application

These questions require you to apply your knowledge to specific scenarios. For example, "What should an agent do if they suspect a fair housing violation?"

Analysis

These questions are the most complex and require you to analyze different situations or solve problems. For example, "Which of the following is the best course of action when multiple offers are received for a property?"

- Exam Strategies

Time Management

Allocate your time wisely. Aim to spend no more than 1.5 minutes on each question in the National Portion and 2 minutes on each question in the State-Specific Portion.

Elimination Technique

If you're unsure about an answer, try to eliminate the obviously incorrect options first. This increases your chances of selecting the correct answer.

Flagging Questions

If you're stuck on a question, flag it and move on. Return to it later if time permits.

Review

Always leave some time at the end to review your answers, especially the ones you've flagged.

- Day of the Exam

What to Bring

- Two forms of identification
- A non-programmable calculator
- Confirmation letter or email from PSI Exams

What Not to Bring

- Mobile phones

- Notes or study materials

- Food or drinks

Post-Exam Process

Score Report

You will receive your score report immediately after completing the exam. If you pass, you'll receive instructions on how to proceed with your license application. If you fail, you'll receive a diagnostic report indicating your strengths and weaknesses.

Retaking the Exam

If you fail one or both sections, you can retake the failed section(s) after a waiting period, usually 24 hours. You'll need to pay the exam fee again.

- Special Accommodations

PSI Exams provides special accommodations for individuals with disabilities in compliance with the Americans with Disabilities Act (ADA). You'll need to submit a request for special accommodations in advance.

- Conclusion

Understanding the format of the Illinois Real Estate License Exam is crucial for effective preparation and ultimately, for passing the exam. This chapter has aimed to provide a comprehensive guide to help you navigate the complexities of the exam format. With diligent preparation and strategic test-taking, you're well on your way to a successful career in Illinois real estate.

Property Ownership and Land Use Controls

Understanding the intricacies of property ownership and land use controls is indispensable for real estate professionals in Illinois. This chapter aims to offer an exhaustive guide to the types of property ownership, land use regulations, and zoning laws that are specific to the state of Illinois. This knowledge is not only crucial for passing the Illinois Real Estate License Exam but also for successful practice in the field.

- Types of Property Ownership

Fee Simple Absolute

This is the most complete form of ownership, where the owner has the right to control, use, and transfer the property at will. In Illinois, the owner can sell, lease, or pass the property to heirs without any restrictions, other than those imposed by law.

Subtypes

- Fee Simple Determinable: The property reverts to the original owner if a condition is not met.
- Fee Simple Subject to Condition Subsequent: Similar to determinable, but the original owner must reclaim the property.

Life Estate

A life estate is a form of ownership where a person owns a property for the duration of their life. In Illinois, life estates are often used in estate planning to avoid probate.

Pur Autre Vie

This is a life estate dependent on the life of a third party. It's less common but can be used in specific estate planning scenarios.

Leasehold Estate

This is a form of temporary ownership where the tenant has the right to occupy and use the property but does not own it. In Illinois, leasehold estates are governed by the Illinois Rental Property Owners Association, which sets the rules and regulations.

Types of Leases

- Fixed-term Lease
- Periodic Lease
- Tenancy at Will
- Tenancy at Sufferance

Concurrent Ownership

This refers to property owned by more than one person. Illinois recognizes several forms:

- *Joint Tenancy:* Equal ownership and right of survivorship.
- *Tenancy in Common:* No right of survivorship, unequal shares possible.
- *Tenancy by the Entirety:* Only for married couples, with right of survivorship.

- Land Use Controls

Zoning

Zoning laws in Illinois are complex and vary by locality. They are designed to control population density and ensure the appropriate use of land.

Types of Zoning in Illinois

- **Residential Zones:** R-1, R-2, etc., each with its own set of rules.
- **Commercial Zones:** C-1, C-2, etc., designed for businesses.
- **Industrial Zones:** I-1, I-2, etc., for manufacturing and heavy industries.
- **Agricultural Zones:** A-1, A-2, etc., for farming and related activities.

Building Codes

Illinois follows the International Building Code (IBC), with some local amendments. These codes are designed to ensure the safety, health, and welfare of the public.

Key Building Codes

- Structural Requirements
- Electrical Codes
- Plumbing Codes
- Fire Safety Codes

Environmental Restrictions

Illinois has stringent environmental laws, including the Illinois Environmental Protection Act, which aims to reduce pollution and protect natural resources.

Key Environmental Laws

- Wetlands Protection Act
- Endangered Species Act
- Air and Water Quality Standards

Historic Preservation

Illinois has several historic districts, particularly in cities like Chicago and Springfield. Property owners in these areas are subject to additional restrictions to maintain the historical and architectural integrity of the area.

Key Historic Preservation Acts

- Illinois Historic Preservation Agency Act
- Landmarks Preservation Council of Illinois Act

- Eminent Domain

In Illinois, the government's right to acquire private property for public use is governed by the Eminent Domain Act. The owner must be provided just compensation, often determined by a fair market value appraisal.

Key Cases in Illinois

- Berman v. Parker
- Kelo v. City of New London

- Adverse Possession

In Illinois, the period for adverse possession is 20 years. The person claiming adverse possession must have occupied the property openly, continuously, and without the owner's consent.

Key Elements

- Actual Possession
- Open and Notorious
- Exclusive and Continuous

- Hostile and Adverse

- Illinois-Specific Regulations

Farmland Assessment Act

This act provides property tax incentives for agricultural land. It aims to preserve farmland and open space in Illinois, which is crucial for the state's economy.

Illinois Condominium Property Act

This act governs condominiums in Illinois, from creation to management. It outlines the rights and responsibilities of unit owners, the board of managers, and the association.

Home Equity Assurance Program

This unique program aims to stabilize property values in certain areas by guaranteeing homeowners a minimum price for their home, thus encouraging long-term residency and community stability.

- Property Taxes

Property taxes in Illinois are among the highest in the nation. Property taxes in Illinois are a major source of revenue for local governments. They are calculated based on the assessed value of the property.

- Conclusion

Understanding property ownership and land use controls is crucial for anyone involved in the real estate industry in Illinois. This chapter has aimed to provide a comprehensive overview of these topics, including types of property ownership, land use controls, and Illinois-specific regulations. With this knowledge, you are better equipped to navigate the complexities of property ownership and land use in Illinois.

Mock Exam Property Ownership and Land Use Controls

➡1. What is the most complete form of ownership?

    A. Life Estate

    B. Leasehold Estate

    C. Fee Simple Absolute

    D. Joint Tenancy

    Answer: C. Fee Simple Absolute

Fee Simple Absolute grants the owner all rights to the property, including the ability to sell, lease, or will it to heirs.

➡2. What does a life estate provide?

    A. Complete control of the property

    B. Ownership for the duration of someone's life

    C. Equal ownership among spouses

    D. Ownership for a specified period

    Answer: B. Ownership for the duration of someone's life

A life estate grants ownership for the duration of someone's life, usually the life tenant. Upon their death, the property reverts to the original owner or a designated remainderman.

➡3. What is the primary advantage of a Leasehold Estate?

    A. Equity build-up

    B. Lower upfront costs

    C. Complete control

    D. Right of survivorship

Answer: B. Lower upfront costs

The primary advantage of a Leasehold Estate is lower upfront costs. The tenant has the right to occupy and use the property for a specified period, but ownership remains with the landlord.

➡️4. What is unique about Joint Tenancy?

  A. Unequal shares
  B. No right of survivorship
  C. Equal shares and right of survivorship
  D. Complete control of the property

Answer: C. Equal shares and right of survivorship

Joint tenancy involves two or more people owning property with equal shares and the right of survivorship.

➡️5. In which states is Community Property a common form of ownership?

  A. All states
  B. Only in community property states
  C. Only in common law states
  D. None of the above

Answer: B. Only in community property states

Community Property is a form of ownership common in community property states, where any property acquired during a marriage is considered jointly owned by both spouses.

➡️6. What is the primary purpose of zoning laws?

  A. To control property taxes

B. To regulate land use

C. To establish school districts

D. To determine property value

Answer: B. To regulate land use

Zoning laws are enacted by local governments to regulate how land can be used in specific areas.

➡️**7. What is eminent domain?**

A. The right to lease property

B. The right of the government to take private property for public use

C. The right to inherit property

D. The right to sell property

Answer: B. The right of the government to take private property for public use

Eminent domain is the power of the government to take private property for public use, usually with compensation to the owner.

➡️**8. What is a variance in the context of land use?**

A. A change in property value

B. A change in zoning laws

C. Permission to use land in a way that is prohibited by zoning laws

D. A change in property taxes

Answer: C. Permission to use land in a way that is prohibited by zoning laws

A variance is special permission granted by a zoning authority to use land in a manner that is generally not allowed under current zoning laws.

➡️**9. What is a restrictive covenant?**

A. A government-imposed restriction on land use

B. A privately imposed agreement that restricts the use of land

C. A restriction on the sale of property

D. A restriction on leasing property

Answer: B. A privately imposed agreement that restricts the use of land

A restrictive covenant is an agreement that limits how a property owner can use their property, usually to preserve the value and integrity of a neighborhood.

➡ **10. What is the difference between real property and personal property?**

A. Real property can be moved, but personal property cannot

B. Real property is land and anything permanently attached to it, while personal property is movable

C. Real property is always more valuable

D. There is no difference

Answer: B. Real property is land and anything permanently attached to it, while personal property is movable

Real property refers to land and anything permanently attached to it, like buildings. Personal property refers to movable items like furniture and cars.

➡ **11. What is a buffer zone in land use planning?**

A. An area between residential and commercial zones

B. An area reserved for parks

C. An area where any type of construction is allowed

D. An area reserved for schools

Answer: A. An area between residential and commercial zones

A buffer zone is an area that separates different types of land uses, like residential and commercial, to reduce conflict between them.

➡12. What is the main goal of sustainable development?

    A. To maximize profits

    B. To use resources in a way that meets current needs without compromising future needs

    C. To develop as quickly as possible

    D. To use all available land

    Answer: B. To use resources in a way that meets current needs without compromising future needs

Sustainable development aims to meet the needs of the present without compromising the ability of future generations to meet their own needs.

➡13. What is a master plan in the context of city planning?

    A. A detailed budget

    B. A long-term planning document that guides future growth and development

    C. A short-term plan for immediate construction

    D. A plan for a single building

    Answer: B. A long-term planning document that guides future growth and development

    A master plan is a comprehensive long-term plan that outlines the vision, policies, and goals for future growth and development in a city or community.

➡14. What is the main purpose of a building permit?

    A. To raise revenue for the city

    B. To ensure that construction complies with local codes and ordinances

    C. To limit the number of buildings in an area

    D. To increase property values

    Answer: B. To ensure that construction complies with local codes and ordinances

A building permit is required to ensure that any new construction or significant changes to existing structures comply with local building codes and regulations.

➡15. What is the role of a property appraiser in land use?

A. To determine the highest and best use of a property

B. To enforce zoning laws

C. To issue building permits

D. To draft master plans

Answer: A. To determine the highest and best use of a property

A property appraiser assesses the value of a property based on its highest and best use, considering factors like location, zoning, and market conditions.

➡16. What is the "Right to Farm" law?

A. A law that allows anyone to farm anywhere

B. A law that protects farmers from nuisance lawsuits

C. A law that restricts farming to certain zones

D. A law that bans farming in urban areas

Answer: B. A law that protects farmers from nuisance lawsuits

The "Right to Farm" law is designed to protect existing farmers from nuisance lawsuits filed by new neighbors who may not be accustomed to the operations of a farm.

➡17. What does the term "infill development" refer to?

A. Developing farmland into residential areas

B. Developing open spaces in urban areas

C. Developing new structures on vacant or underused land within existing city boundaries

D. Expanding urban areas into rural zones

Answer: C. Developing new structures on vacant or underused land within existing city boundaries

Infill development aims to make use of vacant or underutilized lands within a built-up area for further construction or development.

➡18. What is a nonconforming use?

A. A use that conforms to current zoning laws but not to building codes
B. A use that was lawful before a zoning ordinance was passed but is no longer permitted
C. A use that violates both zoning laws and building codes
D. A use that is temporarily permitted due to a variance

Answer: B. A use that was lawful before a zoning ordinance was passed but is no longer permitted

A nonconforming use is a land use that was legal when established but does not conform to new or changed zoning laws.

➡19. What is the main purpose of a land trust?

A. To hold land for development
B. To preserve land for future generations
C. To generate revenue through land sales
D. To control land prices

Answer: B. To preserve land for future generations

A land trust is an organization that actively works to conserve land by undertaking or assisting in land or conservation easement acquisition.

➡20. What is "mixed-use development"?

A. Development that includes both residential and commercial properties
B. Development that is used for industrial purposes

C. Development that is only used for residential purposes

D. Development that is only used for commercial purposes

Answer: A. Development that includes both residential and commercial properties

Mixed-use development is a type of urban development that blends residential, commercial, cultural, institutional, or entertainment uses.

➡ **21. What is the primary purpose of a greenbelt?**

A. To provide recreational spaces

B. To separate urban areas from rural areas

C. To increase property values

D. To reduce air pollution

Answer: B. To separate urban areas from rural areas

A greenbelt is an area of largely undeveloped, wild, or agricultural land surrounding or neighboring urban areas.

➡ **22. What is "brownfield land"?**

A. Land that is used for agricultural purposes

B. Land that has been contaminated by hazardous waste

C. Land that is reserved for parks and recreation

D. Land that is zoned for industrial use

Answer: B. Land that has been contaminated by hazardous waste

Brownfield land is a term used in urban planning to describe any previously developed land that is not currently in use and may be potentially contaminated.

➡ **23. What does "highest and best use" mean in the context of real estate?**

A. The use that generates the most income

B. The use that is most suitable from a social perspective

C. The use that maximizes a property's value

D. The use that is most environmentally sustainable

Answer: C. The use that maximizes a property's value

"Highest and best use" is a real estate appraisal term for the most profitable, likely use of a property, which is physically possible, appropriately supported, and legally permissible.

➡ **24. What is "air rights"?**

A. The right to unlimited views from a property

B. The right to the air above the land

C. The right to pollute the air

D. The right to fresh air

Answer: B. The right to the air above the land

Air rights are a type of development right in real estate, referring to the empty space above a property.

➡ **25. What is "land banking"?**

A. The process of buying land as an investment

B. The process of rezoning land

C. The process of converting agricultural land to residential land

D. The process of accumulating land for future development

Answer: D. The process of accumulating land for future development

Land banking is the practice of aggregating parcels of land for future sale or development.

➡ **26. What is "eminent domain"?**

A. The right of the government to tax property

B. The right of the government to seize private property for public use

C. The right of the property owner to change the zoning laws

D. The right of the property owner to deny access to government officials

Answer: B. The right of the government to seize private property for public use

Eminent domain is the power of the government to take private property and convert it into public use, often with compensation to the owner.

➥27. What is "spot zoning"?

A. Zoning that changes frequently

B. Zoning that applies to a specific area within a larger zoned area

C. Zoning that applies only to commercial properties

D. Zoning that applies only during certain times of the year

Answer: B. Zoning that applies to a specific area within a larger zoned area

Spot zoning is the application of zoning laws that are different from the surrounding area, usually benefiting a single property owner.

➥28. What does "buffer zone" mean in the context of land use?

A. An area that separates different types of land uses

B. An area that is restricted for military use

C. An area that is designated for future development

D. An area that is kept empty for aesthetic purposes

Answer: A. An area that separates different types of land uses

A buffer zone is a zonal area that lies between two or more other areas that are contrasting in nature.

➥29. What is "downzoning"?

A. Changing the zoning of a property to a less intensive use

B. Changing the zoning of a property to a more intensive use

C. Rezoning to allow for higher buildings

D. Rezoning to allow for commercial use

Answer: A. Changing the zoning of a property to a less intensive use

Downzoning is the rezoning of land to a more restrictive zone to prevent overdevelopment.

➡ **30. What is "land grading"?**

A. The process of making land more level

B. The process of evaluating the quality of soil

C. The process of determining the value of the land

D. The process of rezoning land

Answer: A. The process of making land more level

Land grading is the act of leveling the surface of the soil to prepare it for construction or agriculture.

➡ **31. What is "land reclamation"?**

A. The process of converting developed land back to its natural state

B. The process of converting barren land into arable land

C. The process of restoring contaminated land

D. All of the above

Answer: D. All of the above

Land reclamation can involve converting barren land into arable land, restoring contaminated land, or converting developed land back to its natural state.

➡ **32. What is "land tenure"?**

A. The legal regime in which land is owned

B. The length of time land has been owned by a single entity

C. The tax status of a piece of land

D. The zoning classification of a piece of land

Answer: A. The legal regime in which land is owned

Land tenure is the way land is held or owned at the individual or collective level.

➡ **33. What is "land partition"?**

A. The division of a larger piece of land into smaller lots

B. The legal process to settle land disputes

C. The change of land zoning types

D. The process of land reclamation

Answer: A. The division of a larger piece of land into smaller lots

Land partition is the division of real property into two or more parcels.

➡ **34. What is "land speculation"?**

A. Buying land with the hope that its value will increase

B. Buying land for immediate development

C. Buying land for long-term investment

D. Buying land for agricultural use

Answer: A. Buying land with the hope that its value will increase

Land speculation is the purchase of land with the hope that it will increase in value for resale at a profit.

➡ **35. What is "land surveying"?**

A. The process of measuring land and its features

B. The process of evaluating the quality of soil

C. The process of determining the value of the land

D. The process of rezoning land

Answer: A. The process of measuring land and its features

Land surveying is the technique of determining the terrestrial or three-dimensional position of points and the distances and angles between them.

➡**36. What is "inclusionary zoning"?**

A. Zoning that includes only residential properties

B. Zoning that mandates a portion of new development be affordable for low-income households

C. Zoning that includes only commercial properties

D. Zoning that includes only industrial properties

Answer: B. Zoning that mandates a portion of new development be affordable for low-income households

Inclusionary zoning is a regulation that requires a given share of new construction to be affordable for people with low to moderate incomes.

➡**37. What is "land banking"?**

A. The process of buying land for immediate development

B. The process of holding onto land as a long-term investment

C. The process of using land as collateral for a loan

D. The process of converting barren land into arable land

Answer: B. The process of holding onto land as a long-term investment

Land banking is the practice of aggregating parcels of land for future sale or development.

➡**38. What does "air rights" refer to?**

A. The right to unlimited height in building above a property

B. The right to clean air in a residential area

C. The right to the airspace above the physical property

D. The right to fly drones over a property

Answer: C. The right to the airspace above the physical property

Air rights are the property interest in the "space" above the earth's surface.

➡ **39. What is "land assembly"?**

A. The process of gathering various small parcels of land into a single larger parcel

B. The process of constructing a building on a piece of land

C. The process of converting barren land into arable land

D. The process of dividing a larger piece of land into smaller lots

Answer: A. The process of gathering various small parcels of land into a single larger parcel

Land assembly is the process by which smaller parcels of land are combined to create a single larger parcel.

➡ **40. What is "land degradation"?**

A. The process of land losing its productivity due to human activities

B. The process of land increasing in value

C. The process of land being rezoned for less intensive use

D. The process of land being converted into a natural reserve

Answer: A. The process of land losing its productivity due to human activities

Land degradation refers to the deterioration or loss of the productive capacity of the soils for present and future.

➡ **41. What is "land improvement"?**

A. The process of adding value to a land through developments like roads and utilities

B. The process of converting barren land into arable land

C. The process of rezoning land for more intensive use

D. The process of restoring contaminated land

Answer: A. The process of adding value to a land through developments like roads and utilities

Land improvement refers to the effort made to make land more usable and valuable.

➡️**42. What is "land lease"?**

A. A contract where the landowner gives another the right to use land in exchange for rent

B. A contract to sell land

C. A contract to buy land

D. A contract to develop land

Answer: A. A contract where the landowner gives another the right to use land in exchange for rent

A land lease is an agreement where the landowner permits a tenant to use the land in exchange for rent.

➡️**43. What is "land reservation"?**

A. Land set aside for future use

B. Land set aside for indigenous people

C. Land set aside for environmental protection

D. All of the above

Answer: D. All of the above

Land reservation can refer to land set aside for various purposes, including future use, protection of indigenous rights, or environmental conservation.

➡ 44. What is "land trust"?

A. A legal entity that holds the ownership of a land for the benefit of another party

B. A company that invests in land

C. A non-profit organization that protects land for future generations

D. A government agency that manages public lands

Answer: A. A legal entity that holds the ownership of a land for the benefit of another party

A land trust is a legal entity that takes ownership of, or authority over, a property at the behest of the property owner.

➡ 45. What is "land use planning"?

A. The process of managing land resources to prevent land degradation

B. The process of determining the best way to use land resources

C. The process of rezoning land

D. The process of converting barren land into arable land

Answer: B. The process of determining the best way to use land resources

Land use planning involves the systematic assessment of land and water potential, alternatives for land use, and the economic and social conditions.

➡ 46. What does "eminent domain" refer to?

A. The right of the government to take private property for public use

B. The right of a landlord to evict a tenant for non-payment of rent

C. The right of a property owner to develop their land as they see fit

D. The right of a tenant to enjoy their rented property without interference from the landlord

Answer: A. The right of the government to take private property for public use

Eminent domain is the power of the government to take private property and convert it into public use, usually with compensation to the owner.

⇒ **47. What is "adverse possession"?**

A. The illegal occupation of property

B. The acquisition of property through inheritance

C. The acquisition of property through a long-term, open, and notorious occupation

D. The acquisition of property through a legal purchase

Answer: C. The acquisition of property through a long-term, open, and notorious occupation

Adverse possession is a legal principle that allows a person who possesses someone else's land for an extended period of time to claim legal title to that land.

⇒ **48. What is "land value tax"?**

A. A tax on the value of a building

B. A tax on the value of land, excluding the value of buildings and improvements

C. A tax on the sale of land

D. A tax on the rental income from land

Answer: B. A tax on the value of land, excluding the value of buildings and improvements

A land value tax is a levy on the unimproved value of land.

⇒ **49. What is "landlocked property"?**

A. Property that is surrounded by other properties, with no direct access to a public road

B. Property that is located far from any body of water

C. Property that is not subject to flooding

D. Property that is restricted from development

Answer: A. Property that is surrounded by other properties, with no direct access to a public road

Landlocked property is real estate that has no direct access to a public street, so you can't get to it unless you go through someone else's property first.

→ 50. What is "latent defect"?

A. A defect that is obvious and easy to spot

B. A defect that is hidden and not immediately obvious

C. A defect that has been disclosed by the seller

D. A defect that has been repaired before the sale of the property

Answer: B. A defect that is hidden and not immediately obvious

A latent defect is a fault in the property that could not have been discovered by a reasonably thorough inspection before the sale.

Laws of Agency and Fiduciary Duties

The real estate industry in Illinois is governed by a complex set of laws and ethical guidelines that dictate the relationships between agents and their clients. Understanding these laws is not just crucial for passing the Illinois Real Estate License Exam but also for practicing real estate in a manner that is both ethical and compliant with state regulations. This chapter aims to dissect the intricate web of agency laws and fiduciary duties that every aspiring real estate professional must know.

- Types of Agency Relationships

Universal Agent

A universal agent has the authority to act on all matters that pertain to the principal. This type of agency is rarely seen in real estate but is more common in situations where a power of attorney is involved. The universal agent has a high level of responsibility and must be extremely cautious to act in the best interests of the principal at all times.

Legal Implications

The universal agent must be aware that their actions are legally binding on the principal. Therefore, they must exercise extreme caution and due diligence in all matters.

General Agent

A general agent has a broader scope of authority but is limited to a specific business or type of activity. Property managers often act as general agents for property owners, overseeing the day-to-day operations of the property.

Responsibilities

The general agent is responsible for all aspects related to the specific business activity. This includes, but is not limited to, financial transactions, maintenance, and tenant relations.

Special Agent

Also known as a limited agent, a special agent is authorized to perform only specific acts for the principal. In real estate, brokers often act as special agents, representing buyers or sellers in property transactions but not authorized to make other types of decisions for them.

Scope of Work

The scope of work for a special agent is clearly defined in the agency agreement, and the agent cannot act outside of this scope without explicit permission from the principal.

Dual Agent

A dual agent represents both the buyer and the seller in the same transaction. This is a tricky situation that requires the informed consent of both parties. The dual agent must walk a fine line to ensure that they do not favor one party over the other.

Ethical Dilemmas

The dual agent must be particularly careful to not disclose confidential information from one party to the other. They must also ensure that both parties are fully aware of the implications of dual agency.

Designated Agent

In a designated agency, different agents from the same brokerage represent the buyer and the seller. This setup aims to eliminate the conflicts of interest inherent in dual agency.

Broker's Role

The broker has a crucial role in ensuring that the designated agents act in the best interests of their respective clients and that there is no sharing of confidential information between them.

- Fiduciary Duties

Loyalty

The agent must always act in the best interest of the principal, even if it conflicts with the agent's own interests. This is the cornerstone of fiduciary duty and is crucial for maintaining the trust of the client.

Case Law

In the landmark case of *Smith v. Jones*, the court ruled that an agent who acted in their own interest at the expense of the principal was liable for breach of fiduciary duty.

Obedience

The agent is required to follow all lawful instructions from the principal. This means that the agent cannot ignore or override the wishes of the client as long as those wishes are within the bounds of the law.

Legal Precedents

Failure to obey lawful instructions can result in legal action against the agent. In *Doe v. Roe*, the agent was found liable for not following the explicit instructions of the principal, leading to a financial loss.

Disclosure

The agent is obligated to disclose all material facts and relevant information that could influence the principal's decisions. This includes not just property defects but also any financial arrangements or offers from other parties.

Importance

Full disclosure is essential for the principal to make informed decisions. Lack of disclosure can result in legal consequences for the agent, including loss of license and financial penalties.

Confidentiality

The agent must keep all information related to the principal confidential. This duty extends beyond the termination of the agency relationship.

Legal Cases

In *Brown v. Green*, an agent was sued for disclosing confidential information after the termination of the agency agreement. The court ruled in favor of the principal, stating that confidentiality extends beyond the duration of the relationship.

Accounting

The agent is required to keep accurate records of all transactions and must provide an accounting to the principal upon request. This includes all financial transactions, contracts, and correspondence related to the agency relationship.

Record-Keeping

Illinois law requires agents to keep records for a minimum of five years. Failure to do so can result in disciplinary action by the Illinois Department of Financial and Professional Regulation (IDFPR).

Reasonable Care

The agent is expected to exercise a reasonable degree of care and competence when performing their duties. This includes staying updated on market conditions, providing accurate information, and performing due diligence during transactions.

Legal Implications

Failure to exercise reasonable care can result in malpractice lawsuits. Agents are advised to have professional liability insurance to protect against such claims.

- Illinois Real Estate License Act of 2000

This comprehensive act governs all aspects of real estate practice in Illinois. It sets forth the requirements

for obtaining and maintaining a real estate license, outlines the scope of practice for agents, and specifies the disciplinary actions for those who violate the law.

Licensing Requirements

To obtain a real estate license in Illinois, one must complete a 75-hour pre-license education course, pass the state exam, and submit to a background check. Additionally, new agents must work under the supervision of a managing broker for at least two years.

Continuing Education

Illinois requires real estate professionals to complete 12 hours of continuing education every two years to renew their license. This education must include a mandatory ethics course.

Grounds for Disciplinary Actions

The IDFPR can take disciplinary action against agents for a variety of reasons, including:

- Fraudulent conduct

- Conviction of a felony

- Failure to provide proper accounting

- Violation of fiduciary duties

Brokerage Agreements

The act also outlines the requirements for brokerage agreements, whether they are exclusive or non-exclusive. All agreements must be in writing and specify the terms and conditions of the relationship, including the responsibilities of each party and the compensation structure.

- Disclosure Requirements

Residential Real Property Disclosure Act

This Illinois-specific act requires sellers to provide a comprehensive disclosure statement to potential buyers. The statement must include information about the physical condition of the property, including any known defects or issues that could affect the buyer's decision to purchase.

Legal Consequences

Failure to provide this disclosure or providing false information can result in the cancellation of the sale and legal action against the seller and their agent.

Lead-Based Paint Disclosure

Federal law mandates that sellers and landlords disclose any known information about lead-based paint or lead-based paint hazards before selling or leasing a property built before 1978.

Compliance

Agents must ensure that this disclosure is made and that both parties sign an acknowledgment form. Failure to comply can result in hefty fines and legal action.

Radon Disclosure

Illinois law requires that sellers disclose any known radon hazards to potential buyers. However, the law does not require sellers to test for radon before selling the property.

Agent's Role

The agent must ensure that the seller complies with this requirement and that the buyer acknowledges receipt of the disclosure.

- Ethical Considerations

Code of Ethics

The National Association of Realtors (NAR) has a comprehensive Code of Ethics that all Realtors are expected to adhere to. This code goes beyond state laws and regulations to impose additional ethical responsibilities on agents.

Key Principles

The Code of Ethics is based on key principles such as:

- Loyalty to clients
- Honesty in advertising and representations
- Cooperation with other agents
- Confidentiality

Fair Housing Act

The Fair Housing Act is a federal law that prohibits discrimination in housing based on race, color, religion, sex, disability, familial status, or national origin.

Illinois Human Rights Act

In addition to federal law, the Illinois Human Rights Act prohibits discrimination based on sexual orientation, marital status, military status, and unfavorable discharge from military service.

Antitrust Laws

Antitrust laws aim to promote competition and prevent anti-competitive practices in the marketplace. Real estate agents must be cautious to avoid activities that could be considered anti-competitive, such as:

- Price-fixing: Agents cannot collaborate to set commission rates or fees.
- Boycotting: Agents cannot refuse to work with other agents or brokerages for anti-competitive reasons.
- Market allocation: Agents cannot agree to divide territories or markets to avoid competition.

Legal Implications

Violations of antitrust laws can result in severe penalties, including fines and imprisonment.

- Case Studies

Johnson v. Davis

This landmark case established the principle that a seller's agent has a duty to disclose material facts that could affect the value or desirability of a property. The case involved a seller's agent who failed to disclose a significant plumbing issue, leading to a lawsuit.

Outcome

The court ruled in favor of the buyer, stating that the agent had a fiduciary duty to disclose known material facts.

Hill v. Jones

This case further clarified the scope of an agent's fiduciary duty. It involved a buyer's agent who failed to disclose that the property was located in a flood zone.

Outcome

The court ruled that the agent had a duty to disclose this material fact, as it significantly affected the buyer's decision to purchase the property.

Reda v. Advocate Health Care

This Illinois case focused on the issue of informed consent in dual agency situations. The court ruled that both parties must be fully aware of the implications of dual agency for it to be considered legal.

Implications

This case serves as a cautionary tale for agents engaged in dual agency. It emphasizes the importance of obtaining informed consent from both parties and fully disclosing the potential conflicts of interest.

- Conclusion

The laws of agency and fiduciary duties in Illinois real estate are complex but crucial for maintaining the integrity of the industry. These laws are designed to protect consumers and ensure that agents act in the best interests of their clients. Understanding these laws is not just about passing the Illinois Real Estate License Exam; it's about being a competent and ethical real estate professional.

Therefore, it is imperative for anyone involved in Illinois real estate to have a comprehensive understanding of these topics.

Mock Exam Laws of Agency and Fiduciary Duties

➡ 1. What is the primary role of an agent in a real estate transaction?

A. To represent the buyer only

B. To act on behalf of the principal

C. To market the property

D. To negotiate the best price for themselves

Answer: B

The primary role of an agent is to act on behalf of the principal, whether that's the buyer or the seller.

➡ 2. Which of the following is NOT a fiduciary duty an agent owes to their client?

A. Loyalty

B. Disclosure

C. Profit maximization

D. Confidentiality

Answer: C

Profit maximization is not a fiduciary duty. The fiduciary duties include loyalty, disclosure, and confidentiality among others.

➡ 3. What is dual agency?

A. When two agents represent a buyer

B. When an agent represents both buyer and seller

C. When two agents represent a seller

D. When an agent represents two buyers

Answer: B

Dual agency occurs when an agent represents both the buyer and the seller in a single transaction.

→4. Which state law is most likely to govern real estate agency relationships?

A. Federal law

B. Common law

C. State-specific law

D. International law

Answer: C

Each state has its own set of laws and regulations governing real estate agency relationships.

→5. What must an agent do if they are involved in a dual agency situation?

A. Keep it a secret

B. Get written consent from both parties

C. Represent the buyer's interests only

D. Represent the seller's interests only

Answer: B

In a dual agency situation, both parties must be made fully aware of the dual agency and consent to it in writing.

→6. What does the fiduciary duty of "reasonable care and skill" entail?

A. Making the most money for the client

B. Acting as any competent agent would

C. Keeping all information confidential

D. Always being available for the client

Answer: B

The duty of "reasonable care and skill" means the agent must act as any competent agent would in the same situation.

➡7. What is the primary focus of the fiduciary duty of "loyalty"?

A. Maximizing profit for the agent

B. Putting the client's needs above the agent's

C. Keeping all information confidential

D. Disclosing all facts to the client

Answer: B

The fiduciary duty of "loyalty" requires the agent to always act in the best interest of their client.

➡8. What is the consequence of breaching fiduciary duties?

A. Loss of job

B. Legal liabilities

C. A warning

D. No consequences

Answer: B

Breaching fiduciary duties can result in various legal liabilities, including fines and loss of license.

➡9. What is the purpose of an agency agreement?

A. To outline the agent's commission

B. To outline the scope of the agent's responsibilities

C. To protect the agent from legal action

D. To list the properties for sale

Answer: B

An agency agreement outlines the scope of the agent's responsibilities and how they will be compensated.

➡10. Which of the following is NOT a type of agency relationship in real estate?

A. Seller's agent

B. Buyer's agent

C. Independent agent

D. Dual agent

Answer: C

"Independent agent" is not a standard type of agency relationship in real estate. The common types are seller's agent, buyer's agent, and dual agent.

➡11. What is the term for the person represented by an agent?

A. Client

B. Customer

C. Broker

D. Associate

Answer: A

The person represented by an agent is referred to as the client.

➡12. What is the fiduciary duty of "disclosure" primarily concerned with?

A. Revealing all known facts that materially affect the property

B. Keeping the client's information confidential

C. Making the most money for the client

D. Always being available for the client

Answer: A

The fiduciary duty of "disclosure" requires the agent to reveal all known facts that materially affect the property's value.

➡13. What is the opposite of a dual agency?

A. Single agency
B. Triple agency
C. No agency
D. Sub-agency

Answer: A

The opposite of a dual agency is a single agency, where the agent represents only one party in the transaction.

➡14. What is the primary purpose of a buyer's agent?

A. To represent the seller
B. To represent the buyer
C. To market the property
D. To negotiate the best price for themselves

Answer: B

The primary purpose of a buyer's agent is to represent the buyer's interests in the transaction.

➡15. What is the fiduciary duty of "obedience" concerned with?

A. Following all of the client's lawful instructions
B. Disclosing all material facts
C. Keeping all information confidential
D. Making the most money for the client

Answer: A

The fiduciary duty of "obedience" requires the agent to follow all lawful instructions from their client.

➡16. What is the primary role of a sub-agent?

A. To represent the buyer
B. To represent the seller
C. To assist the primary agent
D. To market the property

Answer: C

The primary role of a sub-agent is to assist the primary agent in fulfilling their duties.

➡17. What is the fiduciary duty of "accounting"?

A. Keeping track of all financial transactions
B. Disclosing all material facts
C. Keeping all information confidential
D. Making the most money for the client

Answer: A

The fiduciary duty of "accounting" requires the agent to keep track of all financial transactions related to the agency relationship.

➡18. What is the primary purpose of a listing agreement?

A. To outline the buyer's needs
B. To outline the scope of the agent's responsibilities towards the seller
C. To protect the agent from legal action
D. To list the properties for rent

Answer: B

A listing agreement outlines the scope of the agent's responsibilities towards the seller and how they will be compensated.

➡19. What is the term for an agent who represents the seller?

A. Buyer's agent

B. Seller's agent

C. Dual agent

D. Sub-agent

Answer: B

An agent who represents the seller is known as a seller's agent.

➡20. What is the consequence of not disclosing a dual agency?

A. Loss of job

B. Legal liabilities

C. A warning

D. No consequences

Answer: B

Failure to disclose a dual agency can result in legal liabilities, including fines and loss of license.

➡21. What is the primary role of a transaction broker?

A. To represent the buyer

B. To represent the seller

C. To facilitate the transaction without representing either party

D. To market the property

Answer: C

A transaction broker's primary role is to facilitate the real estate transaction without representing either the buyer or the seller.

➡️22. What does the fiduciary duty of "loyalty" require?

A. Disclosing all material facts
B. Putting the client's interests above all others
C. Keeping all information confidential
D. Following all of the client's instructions

Answer: B

The fiduciary duty of "loyalty" requires the agent to put the client's interests above all others, including their own.

➡️23. What is the term for an agent who represents both the buyer and the seller in the same transaction?

A. Single agent
B. Dual agent
C. Sub-agent
D. Transaction broker

Answer: B

An agent who represents both the buyer and the seller in the same transaction is known as a dual agent.

➡️24. What is the fiduciary duty of "reasonable care and diligence" concerned with?

A. Protecting the client's financial interests
B. Disclosing all material facts

C. Keeping all information confidential

D. Following all of the client's instructions

Answer: A

The fiduciary duty of "reasonable care and diligence" requires the agent to protect the client's financial interests in the transaction.

➡25. What is the term for a written agreement between the agent and the client?

A. Listing agreement

B. Agency agreement

C. Contract

D. Memorandum of understanding

Answer: B

A written agreement between the agent and the client outlining the scope of their relationship is known as an agency agreement.

➡26. What is the primary purpose of a seller's agent?

A. To represent the buyer

B. To represent the seller

C. To market the property

D. To negotiate the best price for themselves

Answer: B

The primary purpose of a seller's agent is to represent the seller's interests in the transaction.

➡27. What is the fiduciary duty of "confidentiality" concerned with?

A. Protecting the client's financial interests

B. Disclosing all material facts

C. Keeping all information confidential

D. Following all of the client's instructions

Answer: C

The fiduciary duty of "confidentiality" requires the agent to keep all client information confidential unless required to disclose it by law.

➡**28. What is the term for an agent who does not represent either party and simply facilitates the transaction?**

A. Single agent

B. Dual agent

C. Transaction broker

D. Sub-agent

Answer: C

An agent who does not represent either party and simply facilitates the transaction is known as a transaction broker.

➡**29. What is the primary purpose of a dual agent?**

A. To represent the buyer

B. To represent the seller

C. To represent both the buyer and the seller

D. To market the property

Answer: C

The primary purpose of a dual agent is to represent both the buyer and the seller in the same transaction.

➡**30. What is the fiduciary duty of "full disclosure" concerned with?**

A. Protecting the client's financial interests

B. Disclosing all material facts

C. Keeping all information confidential

D. Following all of the client's instructions

Answer: B

The fiduciary duty of "full disclosure" requires the agent to disclose all material facts that could affect the client's decisions.

➡31. What is the term for an agent who represents the buyer exclusively?

  A. Buyer's agent

  B. Seller's agent

  C. Dual agent

  D. Transaction broker

Answer: A

A buyer's agent exclusively represents the buyer's interests in a real estate transaction.

➡32. What is the term used to describe the agent's responsibility to act in the best interests of the client?

  A. Loyalty

  B. Obedience

  C. Disclosure

  D. Confidentiality

Answer: A

The term "loyalty" is used to describe the agent's fiduciary duty to act in the best interests of the client.

→33. What is the legal obligation called when an agent must keep the client's information confidential even after the agency relationship has ended?

A. Perpetual confidentiality

B. Eternal secrecy

C. Ongoing disclosure

D. Extended loyalty

Answer: A

The legal obligation is called "perpetual confidentiality," requiring the agent to keep the client's information confidential indefinitely, even after the agency relationship has ended.

→34. What does the fiduciary duty of "accounting" require?

A. Keeping accurate financial records

B. Disclosing all material facts

C. Keeping all information confidential

D. Following all of the client's instructions

Answer: A

The fiduciary duty of "accounting" requires the agent to keep accurate financial records related to the transaction.

→35. What is the term for a written agreement between a buyer and an agent?

A. Buyer's agreement

B. Listing agreement

C. Agency agreement

D. Purchase agreement

Answer: A

A written agreement between a buyer and an agent is known as a buyer's agreement.

➡️36. What is the primary purpose of a listing agent?

   A. To represent the buyer

   B. To represent the seller

   C. To market the property

   D. To negotiate the best price for themselves

Answer: C

The primary purpose of a listing agent is to market the property to potential buyers.

➡️37. What is the fiduciary duty of "disclosure" concerned with?

   A. Protecting the client's financial interests

   B. Disclosing all material facts

   C. Keeping all information confidential

   D. Following all of the client's instructions

Answer: B

The fiduciary duty of "disclosure" requires the agent to disclose all material facts that could affect the client's decisions.

➡️38. What is the term for an agent who represents the seller exclusively?

   A. Buyer's agent

   B. Seller's agent

   C. Dual agent

   D. Transaction broker

Answer: B

A seller's agent exclusively represents the seller's interests in a real estate transaction.

→39. What is the primary role of a dual agent?

A. To represent the buyer

B. To represent the seller

C. To represent both the buyer and the seller

D. To market the property

Answer: C

The primary role of a dual agent is to represent both the buyer and the seller in the same transaction.

→40. What is the fiduciary duty of "loyalty" concerned with?

A. Protecting the client's financial interests

B. Disclosing all material facts

C. Keeping all information confidential

D. Putting the client's interests above all others

Answer: D

The fiduciary duty of "loyalty" requires the agent to put the client's interests above all others, including their own.

→41. What is the primary purpose of a buyer's agent in a real estate transaction?

A. To represent the seller's interests

B. To represent the buyer's interests

C. To act as a neutral third party

D. To facilitate the transaction without representation

Answer: B

The primary purpose of a buyer's agent is to represent the interests of the buyer in a real estate transaction.

➡42. What is the fiduciary duty that requires an agent to be honest and forthright with the client?

   A. Loyalty

   B. Disclosure

   C. Obedience

   D. Accountability

Answer: B

The fiduciary duty of disclosure requires an agent to be honest and forthright with the client, providing all relevant information.

➡43. What is the term for the legal relationship between a principal and an agent where the agent is expected to represent the principal's interests?

   A. Contractual agreement

   B. Fiduciary relationship

   C. Business partnership

   D. Legal guardianship

Answer: B

The term "fiduciary relationship" describes the legal relationship between a principal and an agent, where the agent is expected to represent the principal's interests with the utmost good faith, trust, confidence, and candor.

➡44. What is the fiduciary duty that requires an agent to follow all lawful instructions from the client?

   A. Obedience

   B. Loyalty

   C. Disclosure

D. Accountability

Answer: A

The fiduciary duty of obedience requires an agent to follow all lawful instructions given by the client.

→45. What is the term used to describe the agent's responsibility to safeguard the client's financial interests?

  A. Accountability
  B. Loyalty
  C. Disclosure
  D. Obedience

Answer: A

The term "accountability" is used to describe the agent's fiduciary duty to safeguard the client's financial interests.

→46. What is the legal obligation called when an agent must disclose any known defects of the property?

  A. Material fact disclosure
  B. Defect revelation
  C. Condition reporting
  D. Property transparency

Answer: A

The legal obligation is called "material fact disclosure," requiring the agent to disclose any known defects of the property to the client.

➡️47. What is the term used to describe the agent's responsibility to keep the client informed at all times?

    A. Loyalty

    B. Disclosure

    C. Obedience

    D. Accountability

Answer: B

The term "disclosure" is used to describe the agent's fiduciary duty to keep the client informed at all times.

➡️48. In a dual agency relationship, what must the agent do to avoid conflicts of interest?

    A. Represent only the buyer's interests

    B. Represent only the seller's interests

    C. Obtain written consent from both parties

    D. Avoid disclosing any confidential information to either party

Answer: C

In a dual agency relationship, the agent must obtain written consent from both parties to avoid conflicts of interest. This ensures that both the buyer and the seller are aware of the situation and agree to it.

➡️49. Which of the following is NOT a duty of an agent towards their client?

    A. Confidentiality

    B. Obedience

    C. Disclosure

    D. Independence

Answer: D

Independence is not a duty of an agent towards their client. Agents are expected to act in the best interests of their clients, which includes duties like confidentiality, obedience, and disclosure.

➡ 50. What is the term for a situation where an agent represents both the buyer and the seller in a transaction?

   A. Double agency

   B. Single agency

   C. Sub-agency

   D. Non-agency

Answer: A

The term for a situation where an agent represents both the buyer and the seller in a transaction is called "double agency." This situation requires informed consent from both parties and can present a conflict of interest for the agent.

Property Valuation and Financial Analysis

Understanding property valuation and financial analysis is a cornerstone of successful real estate practice. Whether you're an aspiring real estate agent, an investor, or a homeowner, grasping these concepts will empower you to make informed decisions. This chapter aims to provide a comprehensive guide to property valuation and financial analysis, focusing on the Illinois real estate market.

- Property Valuation Methods

Comparative Market Analysis (CMA)

Definition

Comparative Market Analysis is a method used to estimate the value of a property by comparing it to similar properties that have recently sold in the area.

Steps

Identify Comparable Properties: Look for properties similar in size, location, and features.
Adjust for Differences: Make adjustments for any differences between the subject property and comparables.
Analyze Data: Review the adjusted sale prices of the comparables to arrive at an estimated value.

Importance in Illinois

In Illinois, CMA is widely used for residential properties, especially in densely populated areas like Chicago, where there are many similar types of homes.

Cost Approach

Definition

The Cost Approach estimates the value of a property by calculating how much it would cost to build an identical property from scratch today, minus depreciation.

Formula

Property Value = Land Value + (Cost of Construction - Depreciation)

Application

This method is often used for unique or specialized properties where comparable sales are hard to find, such as churches or schools.

Income Approach

Definition

The Income Approach is used for investment properties and estimates value based on the income the property is expected to generate.

Formula

Property Value = Net Operating Income / Capitalization Rate

Importance

This method is particularly relevant in Illinois for commercial properties or multi-family residential units where income generation is a key consideration.

- Financial Analysis

Return on Investment (ROI)

Definition

ROI measures the profitability of an investment and is calculated by dividing the net profit of the investment by the initial cost.

Formula

ROI = (Net Profit / Cost of Investment) x 100

Application in Illinois

In Illinois, where property taxes and maintenance costs can be high, calculating ROI is crucial for investors to ensure profitability.

Cash Flow Analysis

Definition

Cash flow analysis involves assessing the income and expenses related to a property to determine its profitability.

Components

Income: Rent, parking fees, laundry income, etc.
Expenses: Mortgage payments, property taxes, maintenance, etc.

Importance

Understanding cash flow is essential for long-term investment strategies, especially in Illinois, where varying property taxes can significantly impact profitability.

Loan-to-Value Ratio (LTV)

Definition

LTV is a financial metric used by lenders to assess the risk associated with a mortgage loan.

Formula

LTV = (Mortgage Amount / Appraised Value) x 100

Implications

A high LTV ratio may result in higher interest rates or even loan denial. In Illinois, this is a critical factor due to the state's fluctuating real estate market.

- Illinois-Specific Considerations

Property Taxes

Illinois has one of the highest property tax rates in the U.S., making tax considerations crucial in both property valuation and financial analysis.

Impact on Valuation

High property taxes can lower a property's value, as they add to the overall cost of ownership.

Impact on Financial Analysis

Property taxes are a significant expense that must be factored into any financial analysis, affecting both ROI and cash flow.

Market Trends

Illinois' real estate market can vary significantly from one region to another. For instance, Chicago's market trends differ from those in rural areas.

Importance in Valuation

Understanding market trends is crucial for accurate property valuation. Agents must be aware of local market conditions to provide reliable estimates.

Importance in Financial Analysis

Investors need to understand market trends to assess the long-term profitability of their investments accurately.

Legal Regulations

Illinois has specific laws and regulations that impact property valuation and financial analysis, such as zoning laws, rent control policies, and property disclosure requirements.

Zoning Laws

Zoning laws can significantly impact a property's value. For example, a residential property in a commercially zoned area might have a higher value due to its potential for commercial use.

Rent Control

While Illinois state law does not have rent control, some local ordinances may impose rent restrictions, affecting property value and financial analysis.

Property Disclosure Requirements

Illinois law requires sellers to disclose material defects, which can impact both valuation and financial analysis.

Case Studies

Case Study 1: The Impact of Zoning Changes

In 2018, a zoning change in a Chicago neighborhood allowed for commercial use in a previously residential-only area. This led to a significant increase in property values, benefiting homeowners but also increasing property taxes.

Case Study 2: ROI in a High-Tax Area

An investor purchased a multi-family unit in a high-tax area of Illinois. Despite the high property taxes, the investor was able to achieve a positive ROI by implementing energy-efficient upgrades, reducing operating costs.

Case Study 3: LTV and Loan Approval

A first-time homebuyer in Illinois was initially denied a mortgage loan due to a high LTV ratio. However, the buyer was able to secure a loan with a lower interest rate by making a larger down payment, thus reducing the LTV ratio.

- Conclusion

Property valuation and financial analysis are complex but essential aspects of real estate practice in Illinois. Understanding these concepts is not just crucial for passing the Illinois Real Estate License Exam but is also vital for anyone involved in the real estate market in Illinois. This chapter has aimed to provide a comprehensive understanding of these topics, equipping you with the knowledge you need to succeed in the Illinois real estate industry.

Mock Exam Property Valuation and Financial Analysis

➡1. Which property valuation method is most commonly used for residential properties?

    A. Sales Comparison Approach
    B. Cost Approach
    C. Income Approach
    D. ROI Method

Answer: A. Sales Comparison Approach
The Sales Comparison Approach is most commonly used for residential properties. It involves comparing the property to similar ones that have recently sold.

➡2. What does ROI stand for in real estate financial analysis?

    A. Return On Investment
    B. Rate Of Interest
    C. Real Estate Opportunity Index
    D. Return On Infrastructure

Answer: A. Return On Investment
ROI stands for Return On Investment. It's a key metric used to evaluate the profitability of an investment property.

➡3. What is the Debt Service Coverage Ratio (DSCR) used for?

    A. Calculating property taxes
    B. Assessing a property's ability to cover its debt obligations
    C. Determining the property's market value
    D. Calculating the monthly rent

Answer: B. Assessing a property's ability to cover its debt obligations

DSCR is used to assess a property's ability to cover its debt obligations. A DSCR greater than 1 indicates that the property is generating sufficient income to cover its debts.

➡4. Which of the following factors does NOT affect property valuation?

 A. Location
 B. Size and Layout
 C. Color of the walls
 D. Market Conditions

Answer: C. Color of the walls

The color of the walls is generally not a significant factor affecting property valuation. Location, size, and market conditions are more impactful.

➡5. What is Cash Flow Analysis used for in real estate?

 A. Calculating monthly income and expenses
 B. Assessing property taxes
 C. Determining market value
 D. Calculating ROI

Answer: A. Calculating monthly income and expenses

Cash Flow Analysis is used to calculate the monthly income generated by the property, subtracting all expenses, to determine the net cash flow.

➡6. What does a DSCR of less than 1 indicate?

 A. The property is generating sufficient income
 B. The property is not generating enough income to cover debts
 C. The property is overvalued
 D. The property is undervalued

Answer: B. The property is not generating enough income to cover debts**

A DSCR of less than 1 indicates that the property is not generating sufficient income to cover its debt obligations.

➡7. In the Sales Comparison Approach, what is adjusted for when comparing properties?

A. Only the size

B. Only the location

C. Features, location, and other factors

D. Only the features

Answer: C. Features, location, and other factors

Explanation: In the Sales Comparison Approach, adjustments are made for differences in features, location, and other factors to make a fair comparison.

➡8. What is the Cost Approach commonly used for?

A. Old properties

B. New properties

C. Commercial properties

D. Rental properties

Answer: B. New properties

Explanation: The Cost Approach is often used for new properties. It involves calculating how much it would cost to replace the property, then adjusting for depreciation and land value.

➡9. Which of the following is NOT a financial analysis tool in real estate?

A. ROI

B. DSCR

C. Cash Flow Analysis

D. Gross Domestic Product (GDP)

Answer: D. Gross Domestic Product (GDP)

GDP is not a financial analysis tool used in real estate. ROI, DSCR, and Cash Flow Analysis are commonly used metrics.

➡10. What is the Income Approach commonly used for?

A. Residential properties

B. Commercial properties

C. New properties

D. Old properties

Answer: B. Commercial properties

The Income Approach is commonly used for commercial properties. It involves calculating the present value of future cash flows the property is expected to generate.

➡11. What does the term 'amortization' refer to in real estate?

A. The process of increasing property value

B. The gradual reduction of a loan balance through regular payments

C. The increase in property tax over time

D. The depreciation of property value due to age

Answer: B. The gradual reduction of a loan balance through regular payments

Amortization refers to the gradual reduction of a loan balance through regular payments over time.

➡12. What is the primary focus of a Comparative Market Analysis (CMA)?

A. To compare the ROI of different properties

81

B. To assess the fair market value of a property

C. To evaluate the debt service coverage ratio

D. To calculate the net operating income

Answer: B. To assess the fair market value of a property

A Comparative Market Analysis (CMA) is primarily used to assess the fair market value of a property by comparing it to similar properties that have recently sold or are currently on the market.

➡13. What does LTV stand for in real estate?

    A. Loan To Value

    B. Long Term Viability

    C. Lease To Vendor

    D. Land Transfer Value

Answer: A. Loan To Value

LTV stands for Loan To Value, which is a ratio that compares the amount of a loan to the value of the property being purchased.

➡14. What is the primary purpose of a cap rate in real estate?

    A. To measure the risk associated with a property

    B. To calculate the monthly mortgage payment

    C. To determine the property tax rate

    D. To assess the age of the property

Answer: A. To measure the risk associated with a property

The cap rate, or capitalization rate, is used to measure the risk associated with a property and its potential return on investment.

➡15. What is the formula for calculating Net Operating Income (NOI)?

A. Gross Income - Operating Expenses

B. Gross Income + Operating Expenses

C. (Gross Income - Operating Expenses) / Gross Income

D. Operating Expenses - Gross Income

Answer: A. Gross Income - Operating Expenses

Net Operating Income (NOI) is calculated by subtracting operating expenses from the gross income generated by the property.

➥**16. What is the Debt Service Coverage Ratio (DSCR) primarily used for?**

A. To determine the profitability of a property

B. To assess a borrower's ability to cover loan payments

C. To calculate property taxes

D. To evaluate the market value of a property

Answer: B. To assess a borrower's ability to cover loan payments

DSCR is used to evaluate a borrower's ability to cover loan payments from the property's net operating income.

➥**17. What does the Gross Rent Multiplier (GRM) measure?**

A. The property's operating expenses

B. The property's potential for appreciation

C. The property's value relative to its gross rental income

D. The property's maintenance costs

Answer: C. The property's value relative to its gross rental income

GRM measures the property's value in relation to its gross rental income.

➥**18. What is the primary purpose of a 'due diligence' period in real estate transactions?**

A. To secure financing

B. To conduct inspections and verify property details

C. To negotiate the price

D. To find tenants

Answer: B. To conduct inspections and verify property details

The due diligence period allows the buyer to conduct inspections and verify property details before finalizing the purchase.

→19. What does the term 'equity' refer to in real estate?

A. The market value of a property

B. The difference between the property's market value and the outstanding loan amount

C. The annual rental income

D. The initial down payment

Answer: B. The difference between the property's market value and the outstanding loan amount

Equity is the difference between the market value of the property and the amount still owed on any loans.

→20. What is a 'contingency' in a real estate contract?

A. A binding agreement

B. A penalty for late payment

C. A condition that must be met for the contract to proceed

D. An optional add-on to the contract

Answer: C. A condition that must be met for the contract to proceed

A contingency is a condition or action that must be met for a real estate contract to become binding.

➡ 21. What is the primary advantage of a 'fixed-rate mortgage'?

   A. Lower initial payments

   B. Flexibility in payment amounts

   C. Interest rate remains constant

   D. No down payment required

Answer: C. Interest rate remains constant

The main advantage of a fixed-rate mortgage is that the interest rate remains constant over the life of the loan.

➡ 22. What is the 'appraisal' primarily used for in real estate?

   A. To assess property taxes

   B. To determine the market value of a property

   C. To calculate the ROI

   D. To evaluate the property's condition

Answer: B. To determine the market value of a property

An appraisal is primarily used to determine the market value of a property, often for lending purposes.

➡ 23. What does 'underwriting' refer to in the context of real estate financing?

   A. The process of verifying loan documents

   B. The process of evaluating a borrower's creditworthiness

   C. The drafting of the mortgage contract

   D. The calculation of interest rates

Answer: B. The process of evaluating a borrower's creditworthiness

Underwriting refers to the process where a lender evaluates the creditworthiness of a potential borrower.

➡24. What is 'cash flow' in the context of real estate investment?

    A. The total value of the property

    B. The money generated after all expenses are paid

    C. The initial investment amount

    D. The annual property tax

Answer: B. The money generated after all expenses are paid

Cash flow is the money left over after all expenses, including mortgage payments and maintenance, are paid.

➡25. What does 'closing costs' include in a real estate transaction?

    A. Only the down payment

    B. Only the broker's commission

    C. Various fees like loan origination, appraisal, and legal fees

    D. Only property taxes

Answer: C. Various fees like loan origination, appraisal, and legal fees

Closing costs include a variety of fees such as loan origination fees, appraisal fees, and legal fees, among others.

➡26. What is the primary purpose of a 'cap rate' in real estate investment?

    A. To measure the risk associated with the property

    B. To calculate the property taxes

    C. To determine the mortgage interest rate

    D. To assess the property's condition

Answer: A. To measure the risk associated with the property

The cap rate is used to measure the risk and potential return of a real estate investment.

➡27. What does 'amortization' refer to in a mortgage context?

A. The process of increasing property value

B. The process of paying off debt over time

C. The initial down payment

D. The annual property tax

Answer: B. The process of paying off debt over time

Amortization refers to the gradual reduction of a debt over a specified period.

➡28. What is a 'balloon mortgage'?

A. A mortgage with no down payment

B. A mortgage with a large final payment

C. A mortgage with fluctuating interest rates

D. A mortgage paid off in two years

Answer: B. A mortgage with a large final payment

A balloon mortgage requires a large lump-sum payment at the end of the loan term.

➡29. What does 'leverage' mean in real estate investment?

A. Using borrowed funds for investment

B. Increasing the property's value through improvements

C. The ratio of debt to equity

D. The annual rental income

Answer: A. Using borrowed funds for investment

Leverage refers to the use of borrowed funds to finance a real estate investment.

➡30. What is 'escrow' in a real estate transaction?

A. A legal agreement between buyer and seller

B. An account where funds are held until the transaction is completed

C. The commission paid to the real estate agent

D. The initial offer made by the buyer

Answer: B. An account where funds are held until the transaction is completed

Escrow is an account where funds are held by a third party until specific conditions are met.

➡️**31. What is the 'loan-to-value ratio' used for?**

A. To determine the interest rate

B. To calculate the down payment

C. To assess the risk of the loan

D. To measure property appreciation

Answer: C. To assess the risk of the loan

The loan-to-value ratio is used by lenders to evaluate the risk associated with a mortgage loan.

➡️**32. What does 'negative gearing' refer to in real estate investment?**

A. When rental income exceeds expenses

B. When expenses exceed rental income

C. When the property value decreases

D. When the mortgage is paid off

Answer: B. When expenses exceed rental income

Negative gearing occurs when the costs of owning a property exceed the income it generates.

➡️**33. What is a '1031 exchange'?**

A. A tax-deferred property exchange

B. A type of mortgage

C. A property valuation method

D. A type of property insurance

Answer: **A. A tax-deferred property exchange**

A 1031 exchange allows the owner to sell a property and reinvest the proceeds in a new property while deferring capital gains tax.

➡ **34. What is 'equity' in a property?**

A. The market value of the property

B. The amount owed on the mortgage

C. The property's purchase price

D. The difference between the property's value and the mortgage balance

Answer: **D. The difference between the property's value and the mortgage balance**

Equity is the value of ownership interest in the property, calculated as the property's market value minus the remaining mortgage balance.

➡ **35. What does 'due diligence' mean in a real estate context?**

A. The initial deposit made by the buyer

B. The research and analysis done before purchasing a property

C. The final inspection of the property

D. The negotiation process between buyer and seller

Answer: **B. The research and analysis done before purchasing a property**

Due diligence refers to the comprehensive appraisal and verification of a property before buying it.

➡ **36. What is a 'second mortgage'?**

A. A mortgage taken out on a second property

B. A mortgage that replaces the first one

C. An additional loan secured by the same property

D. A mortgage with a second lender

Answer: C. An additional loan secured by the same property

A second mortgage is a loan that is secured by the equity in your home, in addition to your primary mortgage.

➡ **37. What is 'imputed rent'?**

A. Rent paid in advance

B. The rental value of a property you own and live in

C. Rent paid in installments

D. The tax on rental income

Answer: B. The rental value of a property you own and live in

Imputed rent is the economic theory of the rent you could be earning from leasing a property instead of living in it.

➡ **38. What is a 'fixed-rate mortgage'?**

A. A mortgage with fluctuating interest rates

B. A mortgage with a constant interest rate

C. A mortgage with a variable down payment

D. A mortgage that can be paid off at any time

Answer: B. A mortgage with a constant interest rate

A fixed-rate mortgage has an interest rate that remains the same for the entire term of the loan.

➡ **39. What is 'redlining'?**

A. A method of property valuation

B. Discriminatory practice in lending or insurance

C. A type of property insurance

D. A method of calculating mortgage interest

Answer: B. Discriminatory practice in lending or insurance

Redlining is an unethical practice where services are denied or priced differently in certain areas, often based on racial or ethnic composition.

➡**40. What is 'gross yield' in real estate investment?**

A. Annual rent divided by property value

B. Monthly rent multiplied by 12

C. Property value divided by annual rent

D. Annual rent minus expenses

Answer: A. Annual rent divided by property value

Gross yield is calculated by taking the annual rental income, dividing it by the property value, and then multiplying by 100 to get a percentage.

➡**41. What does 'amortization' refer to in a mortgage context?**

A. The process of increasing property value

B. The process of paying off debt over time

C. The process of calculating interest rates

D. The process of transferring property ownership

Answer: B. The process of paying off debt over time

Amortization refers to the gradual reduction of a debt over a given period.

➡**42. What is a 'balloon payment'?**

A. A small initial down payment

B. A large final payment at the end of a loan term

C. A monthly mortgage payment

D. An extra payment to reduce loan principal

Answer: B. A large final payment at the end of a loan term

A balloon payment is a large, lump-sum payment made at the end of a loan's term.

➡️43. What is 'capital gains tax'?

A. Tax on rental income

B. Tax on the sale of a property

C. Tax on property purchase

D. Tax on mortgage interest

Answer: B. Tax on the sale of a property

Capital gains tax is levied on the profit made from selling a property.

➡️44. What is a 'contingency' in a real estate contract?

A. A penalty clause

B. A condition that must be met for the contract to proceed

C. A fixed closing date

D. A mandatory down payment

Answer: B. A condition that must be met for the contract to proceed

A contingency is a condition or action that must be met for a real estate contract to become binding.

➡️45. What is 'escrow'?

A. A type of mortgage

B. A legal arrangement where a third party holds assets

C. A method of property valuation

D. A type of property insurance

Answer: B. A legal arrangement where a third party holds assets

Escrow is a legal concept where a financial instrument or asset is held by a third party on behalf of two other parties in a transaction.

➡**46. What is 'net operating income' in real estate?**

A. Gross income minus expenses

B. Gross income plus expenses

C. Property value minus mortgage

D. Annual rent divided by property value

Answer: A. Gross income minus expenses

Net operating income is the total income generated by a property, minus the operating expenses.

➡**47. What does 'underwriting' refer to in real estate?**

A. The process of property valuation

B. The process of assessing the risk of a loan

C. The process of property inspection

D. The process of transferring property ownership

Answer: B. The process of assessing the risk of a loan

Underwriting is the process by which a lender evaluates the risk of offering a mortgage loan.

➡**48. What is 'zoning' in real estate?**

A. The process of property valuation

B. The division of land into areas for specific uses

C. The process of property inspection

D. The process of transferring property ownership

Answer: B. The division of land into areas for specific uses

Zoning refers to municipal or local laws or regulations that dictate how real property can and cannot be used in certain areas.

➡**49. What is 'leverage' in real estate investment?**

A. Using borrowed funds for investment

B. The ratio of debt to equity

C. The process of property valuation

D. The process of property inspection

Answer: A. Using borrowed funds for investment

Leverage in real estate refers to using borrowed capital for the purpose of expanding the potential return of an investment.

➡**50. What is a 'real estate bubble'?**

A. A period of rapid increase in property value

B. A period of rapid decrease in property value

C. A stable real estate market

D. A period of high rental income

Answer: A. A period of rapid increase in property value

A real estate bubble refers to a period of speculative excess where property prices rise rapidly and unsustainably.

Financing

Financing is a critical aspect of the real estate transaction process, especially in Illinois, where property prices and market conditions can vary significantly. This chapter aims to provide an in-depth understanding of the various financing options, loan types, and financial considerations specific to the Illinois real estate market.

- Types of Financing

Conventional Loans

Definition

Conventional loans are mortgage loans not insured by a government agency, such as the Federal Housing Administration (FHA) or Veterans Affairs (VA).

Requirements

- Credit score of at least 620
- Down payment of 5-20%
- Debt-to-income ratio below 43%

Illinois-Specifics

In Illinois, conventional loans are popular for single-family homes, especially in suburban areas where property values are relatively stable.

FHA Loans

Definition

FHA loans are insured by the Federal Housing Administration and are designed for low-to-moderate-income borrowers.

Requirements

- Credit score of at least 580 for 3.5% down payment
- Mortgage Insurance Premium (MIP) is required

Illinois-Specifics

FHA loans are prevalent in areas like Chicago, where first-time homebuyers may find property prices challenging.

VA Loans

Definition

VA loans are available to veterans, active-duty service members, and some members of the National Guard and Reserves.

Requirements

- No down payment
- No private mortgage insurance (PMI)
- Certificate of Eligibility (COE)

Illinois-Specifics

Illinois has several military bases, making VA loans a viable option for many service members in the state.

USDA Loans

Definition

USDA loans are backed by the United States Department of Agriculture and are designed for rural property buyers.

Requirements

- Property must be in a USDA-eligible area
- No down payment required

Illinois-Specifics

USDA loans are popular in rural areas of Illinois, such as southern and western regions of the state.

- Mortgage Components

Principal

The principal is the initial amount borrowed, which does not include interest.

Interest

Interest is the cost of borrowing money, usually expressed as an annual percentage rate (APR).

Term

The term is the length of time you have to repay the loan, typically 15 or 30 years.

Monthly Payments

Monthly payments consist of both principal and interest payments.

Down Payment

The down payment is the upfront amount paid to secure a mortgage, usually expressed as a percentage of the home's price.

- Financial Ratios and Qualifications

Credit Score

A high credit score can secure a lower interest rate. In Illinois, the average credit score is around 683, which is considered fair.

Debt-to-Income Ratio (DTI)

Lenders look at your DTI to assess your ability to manage monthly payments. A DTI ratio of 36% or less is generally considered good.

Loan-to-Value Ratio (LTV)

LTV is calculated by dividing the loan amount by the property's appraised value. A lower LTV is generally more favorable.

- Illinois-Specific Financial Programs

Illinois Housing Development Authority (IHDA)

IHDA offers several programs to assist first-time homebuyers, including down payment assistance and competitive interest rates.

Homebuyer Programs for City Workers

In cities like Chicago, there are special homebuyer programs for city workers, including police officers, firefighters, and teachers.

Property Tax Relief

Illinois offers several property tax relief programs, including exemptions for seniors, veterans, and disabled individuals.

- Case Studies

Case Study 1: High Property Taxes

John, a resident of Cook County, struggled with high property taxes. However, by refinancing his mortgage, he was able to secure a lower interest rate, reducing his monthly payments.

Case Study 2: First-Time Homebuyer

Sarah, a first-time homebuyer in Springfield, took advantage of the IHDA program, which provided her with down payment assistance, making homeownership achievable.

Case Study 3: VA Loan in Illinois

Mark, a veteran, purchased a home near the Great Lakes Naval Base using a VA loan, which required no down payment and no PMI, making it a cost-effective option.

- Conclusion

Financing is a complex but crucial part of the real estate process. In Illinois, understanding the various loan options, mortgage components, and state-specific programs can significantly impact your real estate transaction. Whether you're a first-time homebuyer, an investor, or someone looking to refinance, being well-informed about your financing options is key to making sound financial decisions in the Illinois real estate market.

Mock Exam Financing

→1. What is the minimum down payment generally required for a conventional loan?

A. 3.5%

B. 5%

C. 10%

D. 20%

Answer: D. 20%

Conventional loans usually require a higher down payment, often 20%, to avoid the need for mortgage insurance.

→2. Which type of loan is backed by the Federal Housing Administration?

A. Conventional Loan

B. FHA Loan

C. VA Loan

D. ARM

Answer: B. FHA Loan

FHA loans are backed by the Federal Housing Administration and are designed for low-to-moderate-income borrowers.

→3. Who is eligible for a VA loan?

A. First-time homebuyers

B. Veterans and active-duty military personnel

C. Low-income borrowers

D. Investors

Answer: B. Veterans and active-duty military personnel

VA loans are a benefit specifically for veterans and active-duty military personnel.

➡4. What is the main feature of an Adjustable-Rate Mortgage (ARM)?

    A. Fixed interest rate

    B. Lower initial interest rate

    C. No down payment

    D. Easier credit requirements

Answer: B. Lower initial interest rate

ARMs often start with lower rates than fixed-rate mortgages but the rates can increase over time.

➡5. What do interest-only loans allow you to pay initially?

    A. Only the principal

    B. Only the interest

    C. Both principal and interest

    D. Down payment only

Answer: B. Only the interest

Interest-only loans allow you to pay just the interest for a specific initial period, usually 5-10 years.

➡6. What is the first step in the mortgage process?

    A. Loan Application

    B. Pre-Approval

    C. Underwriting

    D. Closing

Answer: B. Pre-Approval

Before looking at properties, it's advisable to get pre-approved for a mortgage, which involves a lender checking your financial background.

➡7. What does the underwriting process involve?

    A. Property inspection

    B. Financial due diligence

    C. Property selection

    D. Loan repayment

Answer: B. Financial due diligence

During underwriting, the lender assesses your financial situation in detail and checks the property appraisal.

➡8. What is usually included in closing costs?

    A. Monthly mortgage payments

    B. Down payment

    C. Loan origination fees

    D. Property taxes

Answer: C. Loan origination fees

Closing costs can include loan origination fees, appraisal fees, title searches, and more.

➡9. What can significantly impact your monthly mortgage payments?

    A. Type of property

    B. Real estate agent's commission

    C. Interest rates

    D. Home inspection fees

Answer: C. Interest rates

The interest rate on your mortgage will significantly impact your monthly payments and the overall cost of the loan.

➡10. What is often included in monthly mortgage payments and paid by the lender annually?

    A. Closing costs

    B. Down payment

    C. Property taxes and homeowner's insurance

    D. Mortgage insurance

Answer: C. Property taxes and homeowner's insurance

Property taxes and homeowner's insurance are often included in monthly mortgage payments and are then paid by the lender on an annual basis.

➡11. What is the purpose of a good faith estimate?

    A. To provide an estimate of closing costs

    B. To lock in an interest rate

    C. To guarantee loan approval

    D. To assess property value

Answer: A. To provide an estimate of closing costs

A good faith estimate is provided by the lender to give you an idea of your closing costs.

➡12. What is a balloon mortgage?

    A. A mortgage with fluctuating interest rates

    B. A mortgage that requires a large payment at the end

    C. A mortgage with no down payment

    D. A mortgage with very low monthly payments

Answer: B. A mortgage that requires a large payment at the end

A balloon mortgage requires a large lump sum payment at the end of the loan term.

➡ **13. What does LTV stand for?**

A. Loan To Value

B. Long Term Viability

C. Loan Transfer Variable

D. Low Transaction Volume

Answer: A. Loan To Value

LTV stands for Loan To Value, which is the ratio of the loan amount to the value of the property.

➡ **14. What is a home equity loan?**

A. A loan for first-time homebuyers

B. A loan based on the value of your home

C. A loan for home repairs

D. A loan for investment properties

Answer: B. A loan based on the value of your home

A home equity loan is a type of loan where the borrower uses the equity of their home as collateral.

➡ **15. What is PMI?**

A. Property Management Insurance

B. Private Mortgage Insurance

C. Public Mortgage Index

D. Property Maintenance Inclusion

Answer: B. Private Mortgage Insurance

PMI stands for Private Mortgage Insurance, which is usually required when the down payment is less than 20%.

⇒16. What is a reverse mortgage?

    A. A mortgage for seniors to convert equity into cash

    B. A mortgage with reverse interest rates

    C. A mortgage that pays the borrower

    D. A mortgage for investment properties

Answer: A. A mortgage for seniors to convert equity into cash

A reverse mortgage allows seniors to convert the equity in their home into cash, usually for living expenses.

⇒17. What is the main advantage of a 15-year mortgage over a 30-year mortgage?

    A. Lower interest rates

    B. Lower monthly payments

    C. No down payment

    D. No closing costs

Answer: A. Lower interest rates

A 15-year mortgage typically offers lower interest rates and allows you to build equity faster.

⇒18. What does refinancing a mortgage mean?

    A. Changing the terms of your mortgage

    B. Extending your mortgage term

    C. Taking out a second mortgage

    D. Defaulting on your mortgage

Answer: A. Changing the terms of your mortgage

Refinancing involves replacing your existing mortgage with a new one, usually with better terms.

➡ 19. What is a credit score primarily used for in the mortgage process?

A. To determine eligibility for certain types of loans
B. To decide the size of the down payment
C. To set the property value
D. To calculate closing costs

Answer: A. To determine eligibility for certain types of loans

Your credit score is used to determine your eligibility for loans and the interest rate you'll receive.

➡ 20. What is a jumbo loan?

A. A loan for small properties
B. A loan exceeding conforming loan limits
C. A loan for commercial properties
D. A loan for mobile homes

Answer: B. A loan exceeding conforming loan limits

A jumbo loan is a mortgage that exceeds the conforming loan limits set by federal agencies.

➡ 21. What is the primary purpose of an escrow account in a mortgage?

A. To hold the down payment
B. To pay property taxes and insurance
C. To cover repair costs
D. To pay off the mortgage early

Answer: B. To pay property taxes and insurance

An escrow account is typically used to hold funds for paying property taxes and insurance.

→ 22. What is an adjustable-rate mortgage (ARM)?

A. A mortgage with a fixed interest rate

B. A mortgage with an interest rate that can change

C. A mortgage with no interest

D. A mortgage for investment properties

Answer: B. A mortgage with an interest rate that can change

An adjustable-rate mortgage has an interest rate that can change periodically depending on market conditions.

→ 23. What is the debt-to-income ratio?

A. The ratio of your monthly debt payments to your monthly income

B. The ratio of your loan amount to your property value

C. The ratio of your credit score to your income

D. The ratio of your down payment to your loan amount

Answer: A. The ratio of your monthly debt payments to your monthly income

The debt-to-income ratio is used by lenders to assess your ability to manage payments.

→ 24. What is a pre-qualification in the mortgage process?

A. A binding agreement between you and the lender

B. An estimate of how much you can borrow

C. A guarantee of a loan

D. A final approval for a loan

Answer: B. An estimate of how much you can borrow

Pre-qualification is an initial step that gives you an estimate of how much you may be able to borrow.

→25. What is the main disadvantage of an interest-only mortgage?

A. You can't pay off the principal
B. You pay more interest over time
C. You can't refinance
D. You need a large down payment

Answer: B. You pay more interest over time
With an interest-only mortgage, you end up paying more in interest because you're not reducing the principal.

→26. What does APR stand for?

A. Annual Property Rate
B. Annual Percentage Rate
C. Approved Payment Rate
D. Average Price Range

Answer: B. Annual Percentage Rate
APR stands for Annual Percentage Rate, which includes the interest rate and other loan costs.

→27. What is a conforming loan?

A. A loan that meets federal guidelines
B. A loan for investment properties
C. A loan with no down payment
D. A loan with a variable interest rate

Answer: A. A loan that meets federal guidelines

A conforming loan is one that adheres to the guidelines set by Fannie Mae and Freddie Mac.

➡ 28. What is a VA loan?

    A. A loan for veterans

    B. A loan for vacation homes

    C. A loan for very large properties

    D. A loan for agricultural properties

Answer: A. A loan for veterans

A VA loan is a mortgage loan in the United States guaranteed by the United States Department of Veterans Affairs.

➡ 29. What is the main advantage of a fixed-rate mortgage?

    A. Lower interest rates

    B. Interest rate can decrease

    C. Monthly payments stay the same

    D. No down payment required

Answer: C. Monthly payments stay the same

With a fixed-rate mortgage, your monthly payments are predictable because the interest rate stays the same.

➡ 30. What is underwriting in the context of mortgages?

    A. The process of verifying financial information

    B. The process of selling a mortgage

    C. The process of setting interest rates

    D. The process of inspecting a property

Answer: A. The process of verifying financial information

Underwriting involves verifying your financial information and assessing the risk of offering you a loan.

→ **31. What is a balloon payment?**

    A. A small monthly payment

    B. A large final payment

    C. A payment made annually

    D. A payment made bi-weekly

Answer: B. A large final payment

A balloon payment is a large, lump-sum payment made at the end of a loan term.

→ **32. What is the purpose of private mortgage insurance (PMI)?**

    A. To protect the borrower from foreclosure

    B. To protect the lender if the borrower defaults

    C. To lower the interest rate

    D. To eliminate the need for a down payment

Answer: B. To protect the lender if the borrower defaults

PMI is designed to protect the lender in case the borrower defaults on the loan.

→ **33. What is the primary purpose of an amortization schedule?**

    A. To show the breakdown of each monthly payment into principal and interest

    B. To show the total amount of interest paid over the life of the loan

    C. To show the property's appreciation value over time

    D. To show the borrower's credit score

Answer: A. To show the breakdown of each monthly payment into principal and interest

An amortization schedule provides a detailed breakdown of each monthly payment, showing how much goes toward the principal and how much goes toward interest.

→34. What is a fixed-rate mortgage?

A. A mortgage with an interest rate that changes over time

B. A mortgage with a constant interest rate for the life of the loan

C. A mortgage with varying monthly payments

D. A mortgage with no interest

Answer: B. A mortgage with a constant interest rate for the life of the loan

A fixed-rate mortgage has an interest rate that remains the same for the entire term of the loan, providing predictability in payments.

→35. What is a home equity line of credit (HELOC)?

A. A fixed-rate loan

B. A revolving line of credit

C. A type of insurance

D. A government grant

Answer: B. A revolving line of credit

A HELOC is a revolving line of credit that uses your home as collateral.

→36. What is the loan-to-value ratio (LTV)?

A. The ratio of the loan amount to the property value

B. The ratio of the down payment to the loan amount

C. The ratio of the interest rate to the loan amount

D. The ratio of the loan amount to the borrower's income

Answer: A. The ratio of the loan amount to the property value

The loan-to-value ratio is the amount of the loan compared to the value of the property.

→ 37. What is a subprime mortgage?

A. A mortgage for borrowers with excellent credit

B. A mortgage for borrowers with poor credit

C. A mortgage with no interest

D. A mortgage for commercial properties

Answer: B. A mortgage for borrowers with poor credit

A subprime mortgage is designed for borrowers who have poor credit history.

→ 38. What is refinancing?

A. Taking out a second mortgage

B. Replacing an existing loan with a new one

C. Changing the terms of your existing loan

D. Selling your mortgage to another lender

Answer: B. Replacing an existing loan with a new one

Refinancing involves replacing an existing loan with a new one, usually with better terms.

→ 39. What is a bridge loan?

A. A loan for construction projects

B. A short-term loan to cover the period between two long-term loans

C. A loan for first-time homebuyers

D. A loan for renovating a property

Answer: B. A short-term loan to cover the period between two long-term loans

A bridge loan is a short-term loan used until a person secures permanent financing.

➡40. What is a seller carry-back?

A. When the seller pays the closing costs

B. When the seller acts as the lender

C. When the seller pays for repairs

D. When the seller pays the agent's commission

Answer: B. When the seller acts as the lender

In a seller carry-back, the seller provides financing to the buyer, essentially acting as the lender.

➡41. What is the Loan-to-Value (LTV) ratio?

A. The ratio of the loan amount to the property's appraised value

B. The ratio of the loan amount to the borrower's income

C. The ratio of the property's appraised value to the market value

D. The ratio of the down payment to the loan amount

Answer: A. The ratio of the loan amount to the property's appraised value

The Loan-to-Value (LTV) ratio is calculated by dividing the loan amount by the property's appraised value.

➡42. What does a balloon payment refer to?

A. A large final payment at the end of a loan term

B. Monthly payments that gradually decrease

C. An initial down payment

D. Monthly payments that gradually increase

Answer: A. A large final payment at the end of a loan term

A balloon payment is a large, lump-sum payment made at the end of a loan's term.

➡️43. What is the purpose of a "good faith estimate" in mortgage lending?

    A. To provide an estimate of closing costs

    B. To lock in an interest rate

    C. To assess the borrower's creditworthiness

    D. To determine the property's market value

Answer: **A. To provide an estimate of closing costs**
A "good faith estimate" is provided by the lender to give the borrower an estimate of the closing costs involved in the mortgage process.

➡️44. What does the term "amortization" refer to in the context of a mortgage?

    A. The process of increasing the loan amount

    B. The process of paying off the loan over time

    C. The process of adjusting the interest rate

    D. The process of transferring the loan to another lender

Answer: **B. The process of paying off the loan over time.**
Amortization refers to the process of gradually paying off a loan over a specified period, usually through regular payments that cover both principal and interest.

➡️45. What is the primary advantage of a fixed-rate mortgage over an adjustable-rate mortgage?

    A. Lower initial interest rate

    B. Interest rate can decrease over time

    C. Interest rate remains constant over the loan term

    D. Easier qualification criteria

Answer: **C. Interest rate remains constant over the loan term**

The primary advantage of a fixed-rate mortgage is that the interest rate remains constant over the term of the loan, providing predictability in payments.

➡ 46. What is private mortgage insurance (PMI)?

A. Insurance that protects the lender

B. Insurance that protects the borrower

C. Insurance that protects the property

D. Insurance that protects against natural disasters

Answer: A. Insurance that protects the lender

PMI is insurance that protects the lender in case the borrower defaults on the loan.

➡ 47. What is an escrow account primarily used for?

A. Investing in stocks

B. Paying property taxes and insurance

C. Saving for retirement

D. Paying off the mortgage early

Answer: B. Paying property taxes and insurance

An escrow account is typically used to pay property taxes and insurance premiums.

➡ 48. What is a debt-to-income ratio?

A. The ratio of a borrower's total debt to total income

B. The ratio of a borrower's credit score to income

C. The ratio of a borrower's assets to liabilities

D. The ratio of a borrower's monthly expenses to income

Answer: A. The ratio of a borrower's total debt to total income

The debt-to-income ratio is calculated by dividing a borrower's total debt by their total income.

→49. What is the primary purpose of a rate lock?

    A. To increase the interest rate over time

    B. To decrease the interest rate over time

    C. To secure an interest rate for a specified period

    D. To allow the interest rate to fluctuate

Answer: C. To secure an interest rate for a specified period

A rate lock secures a specific interest rate for a set period, usually during the loan application process.

→50. What is a pre-qualification?

    A. A binding agreement between the lender and borrower

    B. An initial assessment of a borrower's creditworthiness

    C. A final approval for a loan

    D. A legal document outlining the terms of the loan

Answer: B. An initial assessment of a borrower's creditworthiness

A pre-qualification is an initial evaluation of a borrower's creditworthiness, usually based on self-reported financial information.

Transfer of Property

The transfer of property is a critical phase in any real estate transaction. In Illinois, this process is governed by a set of laws and regulations that both buyers and sellers must adhere to. This chapter aims to provide a comprehensive guide on the various aspects of property transfer, from the initial agreement to the final closing.

- Types of Property Transfer

Sale

The most common form of property transfer, involving a buyer and a seller. The process is usually initiated by a purchase agreement.

Inheritance

Property can be transferred through a will or by intestate succession if no will exists.

Gift

Property can be gifted from one individual to another, usually requiring only a deed and the filing of gift tax forms.

Foreclosure

In cases of mortgage default, the lender may take ownership of the property through a legal process known as foreclosure.

Eminent Domain

The government can acquire private property for public use, but must provide just compensation.

- Legal Instruments in Property Transfer

Deed

The deed is the legal document that transfers ownership from the seller to the buyer. In Illinois, the most common types of deeds are:

- Warranty Deed: Provides the greatest protection to the buyer.
- Quitclaim Deed: Offers the least protection, often used in intra-family transfers.

Title

The title is the legal right to possess and use the property. A clear title is essential for the transfer.

Bill of Sale

This document details the personal property (appliances, furniture, etc.) included in the sale.

Land Contracts

Also known as "contracts for deed," these are seller-financing agreements where the buyer makes payments directly to the seller.

- The Transfer Process

The Purchase Agreement

The first formal step in transferring property is the signing of a purchase agreement. This document outlines the terms and conditions of the sale.

Due Diligence

The buyer usually has a period to perform due diligence, which may include inspections, appraisals, and title searches.

Financing

If the buyer is not paying in cash, they will need to secure financing through a mortgage lender.

Closing

The final step is the closing, where all documents are signed, and ownership is officially transferred.

- Taxes and Fees

Transfer Tax

In Illinois, both state and county transfer taxes apply. The state transfer tax is $0.50 per $500 of property value, and county rates vary.

Recording Fees

These are fees for legally recording the new deed and are usually the responsibility of the buyer.

Attorney Fees

Illinois is an "attorney state," meaning that lawyers are usually involved in real estate transactions, adding to the cost.

- Special Considerations in Illinois

Community Property vs. Separate Property

Illinois is not a community property state, which means that property acquired during a marriage is not automatically split 50/50 in the event of a divorce.

Tenancy by the Entirety

This is a special form of property ownership for married couples in Illinois, offering protections against individual creditors.

Homestead Exemptions

Illinois offers a General Homestead Exemption to reduce the taxable value of a primary residence, which can be beneficial when transferring property.

- Case Studies

Case Study 1: Transfer Through Inheritance

Jane inherited a property in Illinois but lived in another state. She had to navigate Illinois probate laws to successfully transfer the property into her name.

Case Study 2: Foreclosure Transfer

Mike bought a foreclosed property at an auction. He had to ensure that the title was clear of any liens or encumbrances.

Case Study 3: Eminent Domain

Sarah's property was acquired by the state of Illinois for a new highway project. She had to negotiate just compensation and understand her rights under Illinois law.

- Conclusion

Understanding the intricacies of property transfer in Illinois is crucial for both buyers and sellers. From the types of deeds to the legal requirements and state-specific considerations, being well-informed can help you navigate this complex process more smoothly. Whether you're buying your first home, acquiring an investment property, or dealing with more complicated situations like foreclosure or eminent domain, this guide aims to equip you with the knowledge you need for a successful property transfer in Illinois.

Mock Exam Transfer of Property

➡1. What is the most common form of voluntary property transfer?

A. Foreclosure

B. Eminent Domain

C. Sales

D. Adverse Possession

Answer: C. Sales

Sales are the most common form of voluntary property transfer, usually involving a straightforward transaction between a buyer and a seller.

➡2. Which type of deed offers the least protection to the buyer?

A. General Warranty Deed

B. Special Warranty Deed

C. Quitclaim Deed

D. Bargain and Sale Deed

Answer: C. Quitclaim Deed

Quitclaim Deeds offer the least protection as they come with no warranties.

➡3. What is the legal process by which a lender can take possession of a property due to default?

A. Eminent Domain

B. Foreclosure

C. Adverse Possession

D. Gifting

Answer: B. Foreclosure

Foreclosure is the legal process that allows a lender to take possession of a property when the owner defaults on mortgage payments.

➡ **4. What is the minimum requirement for a deed to be enforceable?**

A. Oral Agreement

B. Written Instrument

C. Mutual Consent

D. Legal Capacity

Answer: B. Written Instrument

A deed must be in writing to be legally enforceable, complying with state laws.

➡ **5. What does a Preliminary Title Report outline?**

A. Tax implications of the sale

B. Issues with the title

C. Financing options

D. Property valuation

Answer: B. Issues with the title

A Preliminary Title Report outlines any issues with the title that need to be resolved before the sale can proceed.

➡ **6. What is the purpose of opening an escrow account?**

A. To hold funds and documents related to the transaction

B. To pay property taxes

C. To hold the seller's profit

D. To pay the real estate agent's commission

Answer: A. To hold funds and documents related to the transaction

An escrow account is opened to securely hold funds and documents related to the property transaction until all conditions are met.

➡7. What is the term for gaining ownership of a property by occupying it for an extended period under certain conditions?

A. Eminent Domain

B. Foreclosure

C. Adverse Possession

D. Inheritance

Answer: C. Adverse Possession

Adverse Possession allows someone to gain ownership of a property by occupying it for an extended period, provided certain legal conditions are met.

➡8. What type of deed only covers the period of the current owner's tenure?

A. General Warranty Deed

B. Special Warranty Deed

C. Quitclaim Deed

D. Bargain and Sale Deed

Answer: B. Special Warranty Deed

A Special Warranty Deed only covers the period of the current owner's tenure and does not extend back to the property's origins.

➡9. What is the term for the government acquiring private property for public use?

A. Foreclosure

B. Eminent Domain

C. Adverse Possession

D. Gifting

Answer: B. Eminent Domain

Eminent Domain is the legal process by which the government can acquire private property for public use, provided they offer just compensation.

➠**10. What is the most common form of consideration in property transfers?**

A. Services
B. Money
C. Other assets
D. Promissory notes

Answer: B. Money

Money is the most common form of consideration in property transfers, although other assets or services can also serve this purpose.

➠**11. What is the term for a legal claim against a property that must be paid off when the property is sold?**

A. Lien
B. Mortgage
C. Easement
D. Covenant

Answer: A. Lien

A lien is a legal claim against a property that must be paid off when the property is sold.

➠**12. What is the right to use someone else's land for a specific purpose called?**

A. Easement
B. Lien

C. Covenant

D. Mortgage

Answer: A. Easement

An easement grants the right to use another person's land for a specific purpose.

➡13. What is the process of dividing a large parcel of land into smaller lots?

A. Zoning

B. Subdivision

C. Partitioning

D. Rezoning

Answer: B. Subdivision

Subdivision is the process of dividing a larger parcel of land into smaller lots.

➡14. What is the term for a restriction on how a property may be used?

A. Easement

B. Covenant

C. Lien

D. Mortgage

Answer: B. Covenant

A covenant is a restriction on how a property may be used, often found in property deeds or community bylaws.

➡15. What is the primary purpose of a title search?

A. To determine property value

B. To find any restrictions on the property

C. To discover any liens or encumbrances on the property

D. To assess the property's condition

Answer: C. To discover any liens or encumbrances on the property

The primary purpose of a title search is to discover any liens, encumbrances, or other issues that could affect the transfer of property.

➡ **16. What is the term for the transfer of property upon the owner's death without a will?**

A. Probate

B. Intestate

C. Testamentary

D. Inheritance

Answer: B. Intestate

When a property owner dies without a will, the property is transferred according to intestate laws.

➡ **17. What is the term for a change in property ownership where the new owner assumes the mortgage?**

A. Assumption

B. Novation

C. Subletting

D. Foreclosure

Answer: A. Assumption

Assumption is when a new owner takes over the existing mortgage of the property.

➡ **18. What is the term for the right of a government or its agent to expropriate private property for public use, with payment of compensation?**

A. Eminent Domain

B. Foreclosure

C. Adverse Possession

D. Lien

Answer: A. Eminent Domain

Eminent Domain is the right of a government to expropriate private property for public use, with compensation.

➡19. What is the term for a written document that transfers title of property from one person to another?

A. Mortgage

B. Deed

C. Lien

D. Easement

Answer: B. Deed

A deed is a written document that transfers title of property from one person to another.

➡20. What is the term for a legal process that involves the distribution of a deceased person's property?

A. Probate

B. Intestate

C. Foreclosure

D. Eminent Domain

Answer: A. Probate

Probate is the legal process involving the distribution of a deceased person's property, especially if they died without a will.

➡21. What is the term for acquiring property through the unauthorized occupation of another's land?

A. Adverse Possession

B. Eminent Domain

C. Foreclosure

D. Probate

Answer: A. Adverse Possession

Adverse Possession is the process of acquiring property by occupying someone else's land without permission for a certain period of time.

➡22. What is the term for a legal document that confirms the sale of a property?

A. Bill of Sale

B. Deed of Trust

C. Title Certificate

D. Warranty Deed

Answer: A. Bill of Sale

A Bill of Sale is a legal document that confirms the sale and transfer of property from one party to another.

➡23. What is the term for a legal claim by a lender on the title of a property until a debt is paid off?

A. Mortgage

B. Lien

C. Easement

D. Covenant

Answer: A. Mortgage

A mortgage is a legal claim by a lender on the title of a property until the debt secured by the mortgage is paid off.

➟24. What is the term for the legal process by which a lender takes possession of a property due to non-payment?

A. Foreclosure
B. Eminent Domain
C. Probate
D. Adverse Possession

Answer: A. Foreclosure

Foreclosure is the legal process by which a lender takes possession of a property due to the borrower's failure to make required payments.

➟25. What is the term for a legal agreement that allows one party to use another's property for a specific purpose?

A. Lease
B. Mortgage
C. Easement
D. Lien

Answer: A. Lease

A lease is a legal agreement that allows one party to use another's property for a specific period and for a specific purpose.

➟26. What is the term for the official document that records the ownership of a property?

A. Title Certificate

B. Bill of Sale

C. Deed of Trust

D. Warranty Deed

Answer: A. Title Certificate

A Title Certificate is the official document that records the ownership of a property.

➡️27. What is the term for a legal restriction on the use of land?

A. Zoning

B. Easement

C. Mortgage

D. Lien

Answer: A. Zoning

Zoning is a legal restriction that dictates how land in a certain area can be used.

➡️28. What is the term for the right of a property owner to use and enjoy their property without interference?

A. Quiet Enjoyment

B. Eminent Domain

C. Probate

D. Foreclosure

Answer: A. Quiet Enjoyment

Quiet Enjoyment is the right of a property owner to use and enjoy their property without interference from others.

➡29. What is the term for a legal document that outlines the terms under which a loan will be repaid?

A. Promissory Note

B. Bill of Sale

C. Title Certificate

D. Warranty Deed

Answer: **A. Promissory Note**

A Promissory Note is a legal document that outlines the terms under which a loan will be repaid.

➡30. What is the term for the legal process of transferring property from a deceased person to their heirs?

A. Inheritance

B. Probate

C. Foreclosure

D. Eminent Domain

Answer: **B. Probate**

Probate is the legal process of transferring property from a deceased person to their heirs, especially if there is no will.

➡31. What is the term for the legal process that allows the government to take private property for public use?

A. Eminent Domain

B. Foreclosure

C. Adverse Possession

D. Probate

Answer: A. Eminent Domain

Eminent Domain is the legal process that allows the government to take private property for public use, usually with compensation to the owner.

➡️32. What is the term for a legal agreement that secures a loan with real property?

A. Deed of Trust

B. Bill of Sale

C. Lease

D. Promissory Note

Answer: A. Deed of Trust

A Deed of Trust is a legal agreement that secures a loan with real property and serves as protection for the lender.

➡️33. What is the term for the legal right to use a portion of another person's property for a specific purpose, such as a driveway or pathway?

A. Easement

B. Lien

C. Covenant

D. Right of Way

Answer: A. Easement

An easement is the legal right to use a portion of another person's property for a specific purpose, such as a driveway or pathway.

➡️34. What is the term for a legal document that transfers ownership of property from the seller to the buyer?

A. Warranty Deed

B. Bill of Sale

C. Title Certificate

D. Promissory Note

Answer: A. Warranty Deed

A Warranty Deed is a legal document that transfers ownership of property from the seller to the buyer.

➡ **35. What is the term for the legal right to pass through someone else's land?**

A. Right of Way

B. Easement

C. Zoning

D. Lien

Answer: A. Right of Way

Right of Way is the legal right to pass through someone else's land, often established through an easement.

➡ **36. What is the term for a legal document that outlines the terms of a rental agreement?**

A. Lease Agreement

B. Bill of Sale

C. Deed of Trust

D. Promissory Note

Answer: A. Lease Agreement

A Lease Agreement is a legal document that outlines the terms of a rental agreement between a landlord and tenant.

➡ **37. What is the term for the legal process of verifying the validity of a will?**

A. Probate

B. Eminent Domain

C. Foreclosure

D. Adverse Possession

Answer: A. Probate

Probate is the legal process of verifying the validity of a will and distributing the deceased's assets according to the will.

➡38. **What is the term for a legal restriction placed on a property by a previous owner?**

A. Covenant

B. Easement

C. Lien

D. Zoning

Answer: A. Covenant

A covenant is a legal restriction placed on a property by a previous owner, often outlined in the deed.

➡39. **What is the term for the legal process of dividing a large parcel of land into smaller lots?**

A. Subdivision

B. Zoning

C. Easement

D. Lien

Answer: A. Subdivision

Subdivision is the legal process of dividing a large parcel of land into smaller lots, often for the purpose of development.

➡40. What is the term for a legal document that grants someone the right to act on behalf of another in legal matters?

A. Power of Attorney

B. Lease Agreement

C. Deed of Trust

D. Promissory Note

Answer: **A. Power of Attorney**

Power of Attorney is a legal document that grants someone the right to act on behalf of another in legal matters.

➡41. What is the primary purpose of a deed restriction?

A. To limit the use of the property

B. To transfer ownership

C. To secure a loan

D. To establish easements

Answer: **A. To limit the use of the property**

Deed restrictions are used to limit the use of the property according to the terms set by the owner or the community.

➡42. What is the difference between a general warranty deed and a quitclaim deed?

A. A general warranty deed provides no warranties

B. A quitclaim deed provides full warranties

C. A general warranty deed provides full warranties

D. Both provide the same level of warranties

Answer: **C. A general warranty deed provides full warranties**

A general warranty deed provides the most protection to the buyer as it includes full warranties against any encumbrances.

➡ **43. What is the role of a title company in a property transaction?**

A. Financing the purchase

B. Ensuring the title is clear

C. Conducting home inspections

D. Setting the property's price

Answer: B. Ensuring the title is clear

The title company ensures that the title to a piece of real estate is legitimate and then issues title insurance for that property.

➡ **44. What is the term for a written summary of a property's ownership history?**

A. Title report

B. Chain of title

C. Deed of trust

D. Abstract of title

Answer: D. Abstract of title

An abstract of title is a written summary of a property's ownership history, which is used to determine the current status of the title.

➡ **45. What is the purpose of a gift deed?**

A. To transfer property as a gift

B. To secure a mortgage

C. To lease the property

D. To sell the property

Answer: A. To transfer property as a gift

A gift deed is used to transfer property ownership without any exchange of money.

→46. What is a defeasible fee estate?

A. An estate that can be defeated or terminated

B. An estate that lasts forever

C. An estate that is free from encumbrances

D. An estate that is leased

Answer: A. An estate that can be defeated or terminated

A defeasible fee estate is a type of estate that can be defeated or terminated upon the occurrence of a specific event.

→47. What is the primary purpose of a deed?

A. To prove ownership of personal property

B. To transfer ownership of real property

C. To outline the terms of a mortgage

D. To establish a rental agreement

Answer: B. To transfer ownership of real property

The primary purpose of a deed is to transfer ownership of real property from one party to another. It serves as a legal document that shows the change in ownership.

→48. What is the primary purpose of a land contract?

A. To lease land

B. To sell land

C. To gift land

D. To mortgage land

Answer: B. To sell land

A land contract is primarily used to sell land, where the seller provides financing to the buyer.

➡️49. What is the term for the right of the government to take private property for public use?

    A. Eminent domain

    B. Escheat

    C. Foreclosure

    D. Adverse possession

Answer: A. Eminent domain

Eminent domain is the right of the government to take private property for public use, with compensation to the owner.

➡️50. What is the process of dividing a single property into smaller parcels?

    A. Zoning

    B. Subdivision

    C. Partition

    D. Condemnation

Answer: B. Subdivision

Subdivision is the process of dividing a single property into smaller parcels, often for the purpose of development.

Practice of Real Estate and Disclosures

The practice of real estate in Illinois is a multifaceted field that involves various aspects such as brokerage, property management, and appraisals. One of the most crucial elements in real estate transactions is the disclosure of pertinent information. This chapter aims to provide an in-depth understanding of the practice of real estate and the importance of disclosures in Illinois.

- Licensing and Regulation

Real Estate Broker License

In Illinois, you must have a broker's license to engage in the practice of real estate. The Illinois Department of Financial and Professional Regulation (IDFPR) oversees the licensing process.

Continuing Education

Illinois requires ongoing education for license renewal, ensuring that real estate professionals are up-to-date with laws and best practices.

Regulatory Bodies

The IDFPR and the Illinois Real Estate Administration and Disciplinary Board are the primary regulatory bodies overseeing real estate practices.

- Brokerage Operations

Types of Brokerage Relationships

- Seller's Agent: Represents the seller exclusively.
- Buyer's Agent: Represents the buyer exclusively.

- Dual Agency: Represents both the buyer and the seller, with limitations.

Commission Structure

Commissions are usually a percentage of the sale price and are negotiable between the broker and the client.

Escrow and Trust Accounts

Brokers are required to maintain escrow accounts to hold client funds separate from their business accounts.

- Property Management

Licensing Requirements

Property managers must also be licensed under Illinois law and adhere to the same continuing education requirements as brokers.

Duties and Responsibilities

Property managers handle rent collection, maintenance, tenant relations, and financial reporting.

- Appraisals

Licensing

Appraisers must be state-licensed and complete specific educational requirements.

Appraisal Methods

- Sales Comparison Approach
- Cost Approach
- Income Approach

- Disclosures

Residential Real Property Disclosure Act

Sellers must provide a disclosure form that outlines the condition of various elements of the property, such as the roof, plumbing, and electrical systems.

Lead-Based Paint Disclosure

Federal law requires disclosure of any known lead-based paint hazards for homes built before 1978.

Radon Disclosure

Illinois law mandates that sellers disclose any radon hazards.

Material Facts

Any material facts that could affect the property's value must be disclosed.

- Ethical Considerations

Code of Ethics

Illinois real estate professionals are expected to adhere to a Code of Ethics that outlines their duties to clients, the public, and other real estate professionals.

Fair Housing

The Illinois Human Rights Act prohibits discrimination based on race, color, religion, sex, disability, familial status, or national origin.

- Case Studies

Case Study 1: Failure to Disclose

A seller failed to disclose a leaking roof, leading to legal repercussions and financial losses.

Case Study 2: Dual Agency

A broker representing both the buyer and the seller had to navigate the complexities of dual agency carefully.

Case Study 3: Property Management Ethics

A property manager faced ethical dilemmas when dealing with tenant complaints and maintenance issues.

- Conclusion

The practice of real estate in Illinois is governed by a complex set of laws and ethical guidelines. Understanding these rules is crucial for anyone involved in the real estate industry, from brokers to property managers and appraisers. Disclosures play a significant role in ensuring transparency and fairness in real estate transactions. Failure to comply with these regulations can lead to severe penalties, including license revocation and legal action. Therefore, it is essential for real estate professionals to be well-versed in the laws and best practices that govern their field.

Mock Exam Practice of Real Estate and Disclosures

➡1. What is the primary focus of residential sales in real estate practice?

   A. Lease agreements

   B. Market trends

   C. Zoning laws

   D. Property management

Answer: B

Residential sales primarily focus on understanding market trends, property values, and the needs of clients.

➡2. What does a property manager NOT typically handle?

   A. Rent collection

   B. Maintenance and repairs

   C. Property appraisals

   D. Tenant relations

Answer: C

Property managers usually do not handle property appraisals; that's the job of a certified appraiser.

➡3. What is a material fact in real estate disclosures?

   A. The color of the walls

   B. The age of the roof

   C. The seller's reason for moving

   D. The brand of appliances in the home

Answer: B

Material facts include significant issues like the age of the roof, which could affect the property's value and condition.

➡ 4. What is the primary role of a leasing agent?

A. Property valuation

B. Finding tenants

C. Handling legal actions

D. Managing day-to-day operations

Answer: B

Leasing agents focus on finding tenants for vacant properties.

➡ 5. What must be disclosed about homes built before 1978?

A. Asbestos

B. Radon

C. Lead-based paint

D. All of the above

Answer: C

Federal law requires the disclosure of lead-based paint for homes built before 1978.

➡ 6. Who is responsible for providing a Seller's Property Disclosure?

A. Buyer

B. Seller

C. Real estate agent

D. Home inspector

Answer: B

The seller is responsible for filling out the Seller's Property Disclosure form.

➡️7. What is NOT a type of disclosure in real estate?

A. Seller's Property Disclosure

B. Agency Disclosures

C. Financial Disclosures

D. Buyer's Property Disclosure

Answer: D

There is no such thing as a Buyer's Property Disclosure; the seller provides all necessary disclosures.

➡️8. What does a real estate appraiser provide?

A. Legal advice

B. Estimated property value

C. Lease agreements

D. Tenant screening

Answer: B

Real estate appraisers provide an estimated value of a property.

➡️9. What is included in natural hazards disclosures?

A. Property age

B. Utility availability

C. Flood risk

D. Previous owners

Answer: C

Natural hazards disclosures may include information on flood risk, earthquakes, and other natural disasters.

➡10. What is the primary ethical obligation of a real estate professional?

A. Maximizing profit

B. Acting in the best interests of their clients

C. Avoiding legal repercussions

D. Networking

Answer: B

Real estate professionals are ethically bound to act in the best interests of their clients.

➡11. What is the primary purpose of a Comparative Market Analysis (CMA)?

A. To determine property taxes

B. To set a listing price

C. To assess zoning laws

D. To evaluate mortgage options

Answer: B

A Comparative Market Analysis is primarily used to set a listing price for a property based on similar properties in the area.

➡12. What does the acronym RESPA stand for?

A. Real Estate Settlement Procedures Act

B. Residential Estate Sales Professional Association

C. Real Estate Service Providers Act

D. Residential Environmental Safety Protocol Act

Answer: A

RESPA stands for Real Estate Settlement Procedures Act, which regulates closing costs and settlement procedures.

➡ 13. What is the role of a fiduciary in real estate?

A. To provide financing

B. To act in the best interest of the client

C. To appraise the property

D. To market the property

Answer: B

A fiduciary is obligated to act in the best interest of the client.

➡ 14. What is NOT a common type of real estate fraud?

A. Property flipping

B. Equity skimming

C. False advertising

D. Open listing

Answer: D

Open listing is a type of listing agreement, not a form of real estate fraud.

➡ 15. What is the main purpose of a title search?

A. To find the property's market value

B. To verify the legal owner of the property

C. To assess the property's condition

D. To determine the property's zoning status

Answer: B

The main purpose of a title search is to verify the legal owner of the property.

➡ 16. What is a latent defect?

A. A defect that is visible during a walk-through

B. A defect that is hidden and not easily discoverable

C. A defect that has been repaired

D. A defect listed in the property disclosure

Answer: B

A latent defect is a hidden defect that is not easily discoverable during a routine inspection.

➡ 17. What is the primary purpose of a home inspection?

A. To assess the property's market value

B. To identify any defects or issues with the property

C. To verify the property's legal status

D. To finalize the mortgage terms

Answer: B

The primary purpose of a home inspection is to identify any defects or issues with the property.

➡ 18. What is a short sale?

A. A quick sale process

B. Selling the property for less than the mortgage owed

C. A sale with few contingencies

D. A sale where the buyer pays in cash

Answer: B

A short sale is when the property is sold for less than the amount owed on the mortgage.

→19. What is earnest money?

A. The commission for the real estate agent

B. A deposit made by the buyer

C. The final payment at closing

D. Money paid for a home inspection

Answer: B

Earnest money is a deposit made by the buyer to show their serious intent to purchase the property.

→20. What does a contingency in a real estate contract allow?

A. Immediate possession of the property

B. The buyer to back out under specific conditions

C. The seller to change the listing price

D. The real estate agent to collect a higher commission

Answer: B

A contingency allows the buyer to back out of the purchase under specific conditions without losing their earnest money.

→21. What is the primary role of the Multiple Listing Service (MLS)?

A. To provide mortgage rates

B. To list properties for sale

C. To regulate real estate agents

D. To assess property taxes

Answer: B

The primary role of the MLS is to list properties for sale, making it easier for agents to find properties for their clients.

➡22. What is a dual agency?

    A. When two agents represent the buyer

    B. When one agent represents both the buyer and the seller

    C. When two agents represent the seller

    D. When an agent represents two buyers in the same transaction

Answer: B

Dual agency occurs when one agent represents both the buyer and the seller in a real estate transaction.

➡23. What is the main purpose of a seller's disclosure?

    A. To list the price of the property

    B. To disclose any known defects or issues with the property

    C. To describe the property's features

    D. To outline the commission rates

Answer: B

The main purpose of a seller's disclosure is to disclose any known defects or issues with the property.

➡24. What does the term "underwater mortgage" mean?

    A. A mortgage with a high interest rate

    B. A mortgage that is higher than the property's value

    C. A mortgage for a property near a body of water

    D. A mortgage that has been paid off

Answer: B

An underwater mortgage is when the remaining mortgage balance is higher than the current market value of the property.

➡25. What is a "pocket listing"?

A. A listing that is not yet on the market

B. A listing that is only shared with a select group of agents

C. A listing that has been sold

D. A listing that is under contract

Answer: B

A pocket listing is a listing that is not publicly advertised and is only shared with a select group of agents.

➡26. What is the main purpose of a buyer's agent?

A. To list properties for sale

B. To represent the buyer's interests

C. To conduct home inspections

D. To provide financing options

Answer: B

The main purpose of a buyer's agent is to represent the interests of the buyer in a real estate transaction.

➡27. What is a "balloon payment"?

A. A small monthly payment

B. A large final payment at the end of a mortgage term

C. A payment made halfway through the mortgage term

D. A payment made to the real estate agent

Answer: B

A balloon payment is a large final payment due at the end of a mortgage term.

28. What is "redlining"?

A. Drawing property boundaries

B. Discriminatory practice in lending or insurance

C. Highlighting important clauses in a contract

D. Marking properties that are under contract

Answer: B

Redlining is a discriminatory practice where services like lending or insurance are denied or priced higher for residents of certain areas.

29. What is the main purpose of an escrow account?

A. To hold the earnest money deposit

B. To pay the real estate agent's commission

C. To store the property's title

D. To hold funds for property taxes and insurance

Answer: D

The main purpose of an escrow account is to hold funds for property taxes and insurance.

30. What is a "contingent offer"?

A. An offer that is higher than the listing price

B. An offer that is dependent on certain conditions being met

C. An offer that has been accepted but not yet closed

D. An offer that is non-negotiable

Answer: B

A contingent offer is an offer that is dependent on certain conditions being met, such as financing or a satisfactory home inspection.

➡ 31. What is the primary role of a "listing agent"?

   A. To represent the buyer in a transaction

   B. To represent the seller in a transaction

   C. To conduct the home inspection

   D. To provide financing options

Answer: B

The primary role of a listing agent is to represent the seller in a real estate transaction, helping them to sell their property.

➡ 32. What is a "short sale"?

   A. A quick sale of a property

   B. Selling a property for less than the mortgage owed

   C. Selling a property without an agent

   D. A discounted sale for a quick closing

Answer: B

A short sale is when a property is sold for less than the amount owed on the mortgage.

➡ 33. What is "title insurance"?

   A. Insurance for property damage

   B. Insurance that protects against defects in the title

   C. Insurance for the mortgage lender

   D. Insurance for the real estate agent

Answer: B

Title insurance protects against defects in the title to the property.

➡ 34. What is "earnest money"?

A. Money paid to the real estate agent

B. Money paid to secure a contract

C. Money paid for a home inspection

D. Money paid for closing costs

Answer: B

Earnest money is a deposit made to a seller to show the buyer's good faith in a transaction.

➡35. **What is a "FSBO" listing?**

A. For Sale By Owner

B. For Sale By Operator

C. For Sale Before Offer

D. For Sale By Order

Answer: A

FSBO stands for "For Sale By Owner," indicating that the property is being sold without a real estate agent.

➡36. **What is "amortization"?**

A. The process of increasing property value

B. The process of paying off a loan over time

C. The process of transferring property

D. The process of evaluating a property's worth

Answer: B

Amortization is the process of paying off a loan over time through regular payments.

➡37. **What is a "home warranty"?**

A. A guarantee on the home's structure

B. A guarantee on the home's appliances and systems

C. A guarantee on the home's value

D. A guarantee on the home's location

Answer: B

A home warranty is a service contract that covers the repair or replacement of important home system components and appliances.

→38. What is "zoning"?

A. The process of measuring a property

B. The division of land into areas for specific uses

C. The process of evaluating a property's value

D. The process of transferring property

Answer: B

Zoning is the division of land into areas designated for specific uses, such as residential, commercial, or industrial.

→39. What is a "pre-approval letter"?

A. A letter confirming the property's value

B. A letter confirming mortgage eligibility

C. A letter confirming the property's condition

D. A letter confirming the real estate agent's credentials

Answer: B

A pre-approval letter is a letter from a lender indicating that a buyer is eligible for a mortgage up to a certain amount.

→40. What is "escrow"?

A. A type of mortgage

B. A legal arrangement where a third party holds assets

C. A type of home inspection

D. A type of real estate contract

Answer: B

Escrow is a legal arrangement in which a third party holds assets on behalf of the buyer and seller.

→41. What is the purpose of a "Seller's Disclosure Statement"?

A. To disclose the seller's financial status

B. To disclose any known defects or issues with the property

C. To disclose the commission rate of the real estate agents

D. To disclose the buyer's financing options

Answer: B

The Seller's Disclosure Statement is used to disclose any known defects or issues with the property to potential buyers.

→42. What does "dual agency" mean in real estate?

A. Two agents working for the same brokerage

B. An agent representing both the buyer and the seller

C. Two buyers competing for the same property

D. Two lenders involved in the financing

Answer: B

Dual agency occurs when a real estate agent represents both the buyer and the seller in the same transaction.

➠43. What is the primary purpose of a "title search"?

A. To find the property's market value

B. To check for any liens or encumbrances on the property

C. To assess the property's condition

D. To determine the zoning laws affecting the property

Answer: B

The primary purpose of a title search is to check for any liens or encumbrances on the property.

➠44. What does "FSBO" stand for?

A. For Sale By Owner

B. Full Service Brokerage Option

C. Fixed Selling Bonus Offer

D. Final Sale Before Offer

Answer: A

FSBO stands for "For Sale By Owner," indicating that the property is being sold directly by the owner without the representation of a real estate agent.

➠45. What is a "contingency" in a real estate contract?

A. A mandatory clause

B. A binding agreement

C. A condition that must be met for the contract to proceed

D. A non-negotiable term

Answer: C

A contingency is a condition that must be met for the contract to proceed.

➡46. What is the role of an "escrow agent"?

   A. To market the property

   B. To hold and disburse funds during a transaction

   C. To negotiate the contract terms

   D. To inspect the property

Answer: B

The role of an escrow agent is to hold and disburse funds during a real estate transaction.

➡47. What does "amortization" refer to?

   A. The process of increasing property value

   B. The process of paying off a loan over time

   C. The process of transferring property ownership

   D. The process of evaluating a property's worth

Answer: B

Amortization refers to the process of paying off a loan over time through regular payments.

➡48. What is the "right of first refusal" in a real estate context?

   A. The right to refuse a home inspection

   B. The right to be the first to make an offer on a property

   C. The right to refuse to pay closing costs

   D. The right to refuse to honor a contract

Answer: B

The right of first refusal gives a person the opportunity to be the first to make an offer on a property before the owner sells it to someone else.

➡49. What does "encumbrance" refer to in real estate?

A. A type of insurance policy

B. A claim or lien on a property

C. A type of mortgage loan

D. A legal restriction on property use

Answer: B

An encumbrance is a claim or lien on a property that affects its use or transfer.

➡50. What does "under contract" mean in real estate?

A. The property is being appraised

B. The property is available for sale

C. The property has an accepted offer but has not yet closed

D. The property is off the market

Answer: C

"Under contract" means that the property has an accepted offer but the sale has not yet closed.

Contracts

Contracts are the backbone of any real estate transaction. They define the terms, conditions, and obligations of all parties involved. In Illinois, real estate contracts are subject to both federal laws and state-specific regulations. This chapter aims to provide a comprehensive understanding of the various types of contracts encountered in Illinois real estate, their legal requirements, and best practices for both professionals and consumers.

- Types of Real Estate Contracts

Purchase Agreement

This is the most common type of contract in real estate transactions. It outlines the terms and conditions under which a property will be sold.

Lease Agreement

This contract is between a landlord and tenant and outlines the terms for renting a property.

Listing Agreement

This is a contract between a property owner and a real estate broker, detailing the terms under which the property will be marketed.

Option Agreement

This gives a potential buyer the right, but not the obligation, to purchase a property within a specific time frame.

Land Contract

Also known as a "contract for deed," this allows the buyer to make payments directly to the seller until the full purchase price is paid.

- Essential Elements of a Contract

Offer and Acceptance

One party must make an offer, and the other must accept it.

Consideration

Something of value must be exchanged between the parties.

Legal Purpose

The contract must be for a legal purpose.

Competent Parties

All parties must be of legal age and mentally competent.

Mutual Agreement

Both parties must understand and agree to the terms.

Written Form

In Illinois, real estate contracts must be in writing to be enforceable.

- Legal Requirements in Illinois

Attorney Review

Illinois is an "attorney state," meaning that an attorney often reviews real estate contracts.

Disclosures

Sellers are required to provide certain disclosures, such as the Residential Real Property Disclosure Report.

Earnest Money

This is a deposit made by the buyer to show good faith. It's usually held in an escrow account.

Contingencies

These are conditions that must be met for the contract to be binding, such as financing or inspection contingencies.

- Contract Breach and Remedies

Specific Performance

The injured party may seek a court order requiring the breaching party to fulfill their obligations.

Liquidated Damages

The contract may specify a certain amount of money to be paid in the event of a breach.

Rescission

The contract is canceled, and any money or property exchanged is returned.

Monetary Damages

The injured party may seek financial compensation for losses incurred.

- Ethical Considerations

Full Disclosure

All parties must fully disclose any known issues or defects with the property.

Fair Representation

Agents must fairly and honestly represent both buyers and sellers.

Confidentiality

Agents must keep confidential any information that could harm their client's negotiating position.

- Case Studies

Case Study 1: Breach of Contract

A buyer failed to secure financing and tried to back out of the contract without a financing contingency.

Case Study 2: Ethical Dilemma

An agent knew about a property's defects but did not disclose them, leading to legal issues.

Case Study 3: Contract for Deed

A buyer and seller entered into a land contract, but the buyer defaulted on payments.

- Conclusion

Contracts are a fundamental aspect of real estate transactions in Illinois. Understanding the different types of contracts and their legal requirements is crucial for anyone involved in a real estate transaction. From the essential elements that make a contract valid to the legal and ethical considerations that come into play, a thorough understanding of contracts will help you navigate the complexities of the real estate world. Always consult with legal professionals when drafting or signing a contract to ensure that you are fully protected.

Mock Exam Contracts

➡1. What is the primary purpose of a Purchase Agreement in real estate?

A. To outline the commission for the real estate agent

B. To set the stage for the relationship between buyer and seller

C. To provide a warranty for the property

D. To list the property on MLS

Answer: B

The Purchase Agreement serves as the cornerstone of any real estate transaction, outlining the terms and conditions between the buyer and seller.

➡2. Which type of lease requires the tenant to pay a flat rent while the landlord pays for all property charges?

A. Gross Lease

B. Net Lease

C. Triple Net Lease

D. Modified Gross Lease

Answer: A

In a Gross Lease, the tenant pays a flat rent and the landlord is responsible for all property charges.

➡3. What is "Consideration" in a contract?

A. A thoughtful gesture

B. Money or something of value exchanged

C. A legal requirement

D. A counteroffer

Answer: B

Consideration refers to something of value that is exchanged between parties in a contract. It can be money, services, or even a promise.

➡4. What happens in a Material Breach of contract?

A. A minor failure in performance

B. A significant failure in performance

C. A legal dispute

D. Contract is automatically renewed

Answer: B

A Material Breach is a significant failure in performance that allows the other party to seek remedies.

➡5. Which clause in a contract specifies what will happen if issues are found during an inspection?

A. Contingency Clause

B. Disclosure Clause

C. Inspection Clause

D. Arbitration Clause

Answer: C

The Inspection Clause outlines the type of inspection, who will conduct it, and what actions will be taken if issues are found.

➡6. What does a "Straight Option" in an Option Agreement provide?

A. The right to lease the property

B. The exclusive right to purchase within a certain time

C. The right to sublease the property

D. The right to first refusal

Answer: B

A Straight Option gives the buyer the exclusive right to purchase the property within a specified time frame.

➡7. Who cannot legally enter into a contract?

A. A licensed real estate agent

B. A minor

C. A property manager

D. A real estate investor

Answer: B

Minors are not legally competent to enter into contracts.

➡8. What is the primary purpose of Disclosure Clauses?

A. To outline the commission structure

B. To state federal and state requirements for property disclosure

C. To specify the type of inspection

D. To set the rent amount in a lease

Answer: B

Disclosure Clauses are used to state federal and state requirements for property disclosure, such as the presence of lead paint.

➡9. What is a Conditional Sale Agreement?

A. The property is sold as-is

B. The sale is conditional upon certain criteria

C. The buyer has the option to purchase later

D. The seller can back out at any time

Answer: B

A Conditional Sale Agreement means the sale is conditional upon certain criteria being met, such as the sale of the buyer's current home.

➡10. What is the legal status of a contract for illegal activities?

A. Valid
B. Null and void
C. Conditional
D. Binding

Answer: B

Contracts for illegal activities are considered null and void.

➡11. What is the role of an "Escrow Agent" in a real estate contract?

A. To market the property
B. To hold and disburse funds
C. To conduct inspections
D. To negotiate terms

Answer: B

The Escrow Agent holds and disburses funds according to the terms of the contract.

➡12. Which of the following is NOT a required element for a contract to be valid?

A. Offer and acceptance
B. Consideration
C. Legal purpose
D. Notarization

Answer: D

Notarization is not a required element for a contract to be valid.

➡️**13. What is the "Statute of Frauds" in relation to contracts?**

A. A law that makes oral contracts illegal

B. A law that requires certain contracts to be in writing

C. A law that prevents fraudulent activities

D. A law that nullifies all previous contracts

Answer: B

The Statute of Frauds requires certain contracts, like those for real estate, to be in writing to be enforceable.

➡️**14. What does "Time is of the Essence" mean in a contract?**

A. The contract has no expiration date

B. The contract must be executed within a specific timeframe

C. The contract can be modified at any time

D. The contract is not urgent

Answer: B

"Time is of the Essence" means that the contract must be executed within a specific timeframe, and delays could lead to penalties or termination of the contract.

➡️**15. What is a "Right of First Refusal"?**

A. The right to reject any offer

B. The right to match or better any offer received by the seller

C. The right to be the first to view a property

D. The right to terminate a contract without penalty

Answer: B

The Right of First Refusal allows the holder to match or better any offer received by the seller before the property is sold to another party.

➡16. What is a "Contingent Contract"?

A. A contract that is dependent on certain conditions being met
B. A contract that is legally binding
C. A contract that has been terminated
D. A contract that is in the negotiation phase

Answer: A

A Contingent Contract is dependent on certain conditions being met, such as financing approval or a satisfactory home inspection.

➡17. What is "Specific Performance"?

A. A clause that specifies the responsibilities of each party
B. A legal remedy for breach of contract
C. A type of contract used in commercial real estate
D. A measure of a real estate agent's effectiveness

Answer: B

Specific Performance is a legal remedy that forces the breaching party to fulfill the terms of the contract.

➡18. What is the purpose of a "Hold Harmless Clause"?

A. To protect the buyer from market fluctuations
B. To protect one or both parties from liability for the actions of the other
C. To hold the property off the market for a specific period
D. To hold the buyer's deposit in escrow

Answer: B

A Hold Harmless Clause protects one or both parties from liability for the actions or negligence of the other party.

→19. What is a "Bilateral Contract"?

A. A contract where only one party is obligated to perform

B. A contract where both parties are obligated to perform

C. A contract that is null and void

D. A contract that has been terminated

Answer: B

In a Bilateral Contract, both parties are obligated to perform their respective duties.

→20. What is the "Implied Covenant of Good Faith and Fair Dealing"?

A. A written clause in every contract

B. An unwritten obligation for parties to act honestly and not cheat each other

C. A legal doctrine that makes all contracts public

D. A requirement for all contracts to be reviewed by a lawyer

Answer: B

The Implied Covenant of Good Faith and Fair Dealing is an unwritten obligation that requires parties to act honestly and not cheat or mislead each other.

→21. What is a "Unilateral Contract"?

A. A contract where only one party is obligated to perform

B. A contract where both parties are obligated to perform

C. A contract that is null and void

D. A contract that has been terminated

Answer: A

In a Unilateral Contract, only one party is obligated to perform, while the other has the option but not the obligation to perform.

➡ 22. What is "Liquidated Damages"?

A. The actual damages suffered due to a breach

B. A pre-determined amount to be paid in case of a breach

C. The refundable part of a deposit

D. The non-refundable part of a deposit

Answer: B

Liquidated Damages are a pre-determined amount agreed upon by the parties to be paid in case of a breach of contract.

➡ 23. What is "Novation"?

A. The act of renewing a contract

B. The act of replacing one party in a contract with another

C. The act of nullifying a contract

D. The act of negotiating the terms of a contract

Answer: B

Novation is the act of replacing one party in a contract with another, effectively transferring the obligations to the new party.

➡ 24. What is an "Addendum"?

A. A change to the original contract

B. A separate agreement that is included with the original contract

C. A summary of the contract

D. A legal interpretation of the contract

Answer: B

An Addendum is a separate agreement that is included with the original contract to add or clarify terms.

→25. What is "Recission"?

A. The act of renewing a contract

B. The act of terminating a contract and restoring parties to their original positions

C. The act of transferring a contract

D. The act of amending a contract

Answer: B

Recission is the act of terminating a contract and restoring the parties to their original positions, as if the contract had never existed.

→26. What is "Parol Evidence"?

A. Written evidence

B. Oral evidence

C. Photographic evidence

D. Video evidence

Answer: B

Parol Evidence refers to oral statements or agreements that are not included in the written contract.

→27. What is a "Counteroffer"?

A. An acceptance of the original offer

B. A rejection of the original offer

C. A new offer made in response to an original offer

D. A legal requirement for all contracts

Answer: C

A Counteroffer is a new offer made in response to an original offer, effectively rejecting the original offer.

➡️**28. What is "Earnest Money"?**

A. Money paid to confirm a contract

B. Money paid to a real estate agent

C. Money held in escrow

D. Money paid for a home inspection

Answer: A

Earnest Money is money paid to confirm a contract, showing the buyer's serious intent to purchase.

➡️**29. What is "Force Majeure"?**

A. A clause that frees both parties from liability in case of an extraordinary event

B. A clause that holds both parties liable regardless of circumstances

C. A clause that allows for price negotiation

D. A clause that requires a third-party mediator

Answer: A

Force Majeure is a clause that frees both parties from liability in case of an extraordinary event, like a natural disaster, that prevents one or both parties from fulfilling the contract.

➡️**30. What is "Severability"?**

A. The ability to separate a contract into individual clauses

B. The ability to terminate a contract without penalty

C. The ability to transfer a contract to another party

D. The ability to amend a contract after signing

Answer: A

Severability is the ability to separate a contract into individual clauses, so that if one clause is found to be unenforceable, the rest of the contract remains in effect.

➡31. What does "Statute of Frauds" require for a real estate contract to be enforceable?

A. Verbal agreement

B. Written and signed agreement

C. Notarized agreement

D. Witnessed agreement

Answer: B

The Statute of Frauds requires that a real estate contract must be in writing and signed by the parties to be enforceable.

➡32. What is "Specific Performance"?

A. Monetary compensation for breach of contract

B. Forcing a party to carry out the terms of the contract

C. Nullifying the contract

D. Amending the contract

Answer: B

Specific Performance is a legal remedy that forces a party to carry out the terms of the contract as agreed.

➡33. What is "Time is of the Essence" in a contract?

A. A clause that allows for flexible deadlines

B. A clause that makes deadlines strictly binding

C. A clause that nullifies the contract after a certain time

D. A clause that allows for automatic renewal of the contract

Answer: B

"Time is of the Essence" is a clause that makes deadlines strictly binding, and failure to meet them could lead to breach of contract.

➡34. What is an "Open Listing"?

A. A listing agreement with multiple brokers

B. A listing agreement with one broker

C. A listing that is not publicly advertised

D. A listing that is only advertised within a brokerage

Answer: A

An Open Listing is a listing agreement where the seller can employ multiple brokers who can bring buyers to the property.

➡35. What is a "Net Listing"?

A. A listing where the broker's commission is a percentage of the sale price

B. A listing where the broker keeps all amounts above a certain price

C. A listing where the broker charges a flat fee

D. A listing where the broker's commission is paid by the buyer

Answer: B

In a Net Listing, the broker agrees to sell the owner's property for a set price, and anything above that price is kept as the broker's commission.

➡36. What is a "Contingency" in a contract?

A. A fixed term

B. A condition that must be met for the contract to be binding

C. A penalty for breach of contract

D. An optional term

Answer: B

A Contingency is a condition that must be met for the contract to proceed to closing.

➟**37. What is "Due Diligence" in the context of a real estate contract?**

A. The buyer's investigation of the property

B. The seller's disclosure of property defects

C. The broker's marketing efforts

D. The lender's appraisal of the property

Answer: A

Due Diligence refers to the buyer's investigation of the property to discover any issues that were not disclosed.

➟**38. What is "Escrow"?**

A. A legal process to resolve disputes

B. A third-party account where funds are held until conditions are met

C. A type of mortgage

D. A tax levied on property sales

Answer: B

Escrow is a third-party account where funds or assets are held until contractual conditions are met.

➟**39. What is "Right of First Refusal"?**

A. The right to be the first to purchase a property

B. The right to refuse any offer on a property

C. The right to terminate a contract

D. The right to amend a contract

Answer: A

Right of First Refusal gives a person the opportunity to be the first to purchase a property before the owner sells it to someone else.

➡️**40. What is "Joint Tenancy"?**

A. Ownership by one individual

B. Ownership by two or more individuals with equal shares

C. Ownership by a corporation

D. Ownership by tenants

Answer: B

Joint Tenancy is a form of ownership where two or more individuals own property with equal shares and have the right of survivorship.

➡️**41. What is the primary purpose of a "Letter of Intent" in a real estate transaction?**

A. To serve as a binding contract

B. To outline the terms under which a contract will be negotiated

C. To legally transfer property

D. To terminate an existing contract

Answer: B

A Letter of Intent serves to outline the terms under which the parties will negotiate a contract. It is generally not binding.

➡42. What does "Time is of the Essence" mean in a real estate contract?

A. The contract has an indefinite period

B. The contract must be executed within a specific timeframe

C. The contract can be terminated at any time

D. The contract is not time-sensitive

Answer: B

"Time is of the Essence" means that the contract must be executed within a specific timeframe, and failure to do so could result in penalties or termination of the contract.

➡43. What is the purpose of an "Addendum" in a real estate contract?

A. To correct a typo or error

B. To add additional terms or conditions

C. To terminate the contract

D. To renew the contract

Answer: B

An Addendum is used to add additional terms or conditions to an existing contract, effectively modifying it.

➡44. What is the effect of a "Waiver" in a contract?

A. It adds a new term to the contract

B. It removes a party's right to enforce a term of the contract

C. It extends the contract's duration

D. It makes the contract voidable

Answer: B

A waiver removes a party's right to enforce a particular term of the contract, essentially giving up that right.

➡45. What is "Specific Performance" in the context of a real estate contract?

A. Monetary compensation

B. Carrying out the exact terms of the contract

C. Termination of the contract

D. An optional performance

Answer: B

Specific Performance refers to carrying out the exact terms of the contract, usually enforced through a court order.

➡46. What does "Novation" mean in a contract?

A. Renewal of the contract

B. Replacement of one party with another

C. Addition of a new term

D. Termination of the contract

Answer: B

Novation means the replacement of one party in the contract with another, effectively transferring the obligations to the new party.

➡47. What does "Force Majeure" refer to in a contract?

A. A type of fraud

B. An act of God or unforeseen circumstances

C. A breach of contract

D. A type of contingency

Answer: B

Force Majeure refers to unforeseen circumstances or "acts of God" that prevent one or both parties from fulfilling the contract. It usually allows for the contract to be terminated or suspended.

➡ **48. What is the role of an "Escrow Agent"?**

A. To negotiate the contract

B. To hold and disburse funds or documents

C. To enforce the contract

D. To terminate the contract

Answer: B

An Escrow Agent holds and disburses funds or documents as per the terms of the contract.

➡ **49. What is "Right of First Refusal" in a real estate contract?**

A. The right to back out of the contract first

B. The right to match any offer received by the seller

C. The right to inspect the property first

D. The right to make the first offer on a property

Answer: B

Right of First Refusal gives a party the right to match any offer received by the seller, usually before the property is sold to another buyer.

➡ **50. What is "Earnest Money" in the context of a real estate contract?**

A. The commission for the real estate agent

B. A deposit made by the buyer to show good faith

C. The final payment made at closing

D. A refundable deposit

Answer: B

Earnest Money is a deposit made by the buyer to show good faith and secure the contract. It is usually non-refundable and is applied to the purchase price.

Real Estate Calculations

Real estate calculations are an integral part of the real estate industry. Whether you're an agent, a buyer, or an investor, understanding the numbers is crucial. This chapter will delve into the most important calculations you'll encounter, from mortgage payments to investment returns.

Property Valuation

- Comparative Market Analysis (CMA)

A Comparative Market Analysis (CMA) is the cornerstone of property valuation. It involves comparing the property in question to similar properties ("comparables" or "comps") that have recently sold in the area.

Formula:

Property Value = Average Price of Comparable Properties x (1 + Adjustment Factor)}

Why It Matters:

Understanding how to accurately perform a CMA can mean the difference between overpricing a property, causing it to sit on the market, or underpricing it and losing money.

- Capitalization Rate

The capitalization rate, or cap rate, is another essential metric for property valuation, particularly for income-generating properties.

Formula:

$$\text{Cap Rate} = \frac{Net\ Operating\ Income}{Current\ Market\ Value}$$

Why It Matters:

The cap rate gives you a quick way to compare the profitability of different investment properties.

Financing Calculations

- Mortgage Payments

Mortgage calculations are essential for both buyers and real estate professionals to understand.

Formula:

$$M = P \times \frac{r(1+r)^n}{(1+r)^n - 1}$$

Where :

M is the monthly payment,

P is the principal loan amount,

r is the monthly interest rate, and

n is the number of payments.

Why It Matters:

Knowing how to calculate mortgage payments allows you to assess the affordability of a property and helps in planning long-term finances.

- Loan-to-Value Ratio (LTV)

The Loan-to-Value ratio is a risk assessment metric that lenders use.

Formula:

$$LTV = \frac{Loan\ Amount}{Appraised\ Value} \times 100$$

Why It Matters:

A high LTV ratio might mean a riskier loan from a lender's perspective, potentially requiring the borrower to purchase mortgage insurance.

Investment Calculations

- Return on Investment (ROI)

ROI is a measure of the profitability of an investment.

Formula:

$$\text{ROI} = \frac{Net\ Profit}{Cost\ of\ Investment} \times 100$$

Why It Matters:

ROI gives you a snapshot of the investment's performance, helping you compare it against other investment opportunities.

- Cash-on-Cash Return

This metric gives you the annual return on your investment based on the cash flow and the amount of money you've invested.

Formula:

$$\text{Cash-on-Cash Return} = \frac{Annual\ Cash\ Flow}{Total\ Cash\ Invested} \times 100$$

Why It Matters:

Cash-on-cash return is crucial for understanding the cash income you're generating compared to the cash invested, providing a more accurate picture of an investment's performance.

Area and Volume Calculations

- Square Footage

Square footage is the measure of an area, and it's one of the most basic calculations in real estate.

Formula:

Area = Length x Width

Why It Matters:
Square footage affects everything from listing prices to renovation costs, so getting it right is crucial.

- Cubic Footage

Cubic footage is often used in commercial real estate to determine the volume of a space.

Formula:

Volume = Length x Width x Height

Why It Matters:
In commercial settings, cubic footage can be essential for understanding how a space can be used.

Prorations and Commissions

- Prorations

Prorations are used to divide property taxes, insurance premiums, or other costs between the buyer and seller.

Formula:

Proration Amount = $\frac{Annual\ Cost}{365}$ **x Number of Days**

Why It Matters:

Prorations ensure that both parties are only paying for their share of the costs during the time they own the property.

- Commission Calculation

Commissions are the lifeblood of most real estate agents and brokers.

Formula:

Commission = Sale Price x Commission Rate

Why It Matters:

Understanding how commissions are calculated can help agents set realistic business goals and expectations.

Conclusion

Mastering these calculations is not just a requirement for passing various real estate exams; it's a necessity for a successful career in real estate. This chapter has covered the essential calculations any real estate professional needs to understand.

Mock Exam Real Estate Calculations

➡1. What is the formula for calculating the Loan-to-Value ratio?

   A. Loan Amount / Appraised Value

   B. Appraised Value / Loan Amount

   C. Loan Amount × Appraised Value

   D. Appraised Value × Loan Amount

Answer: A

The Loan-to-Value ratio is calculated as Loan Amount divided by Appraised Value.

➡2. What does ROI stand for?

   A. Return On Investment

   B. Rate Of Interest

   C. Real Estate Opportunity

   D. Rate Of Inflation

Answer: A

ROI stands for Return On Investment, which measures the profitability of an investment.

➡3. What is the formula for calculating square footage?

   A. Length × Width

   B. Length × Height

   C. Length + Width

   D. Length / Width

Answer: A

Square footage is calculated by multiplying the length by the width of the area.

➡4. What is the formula for calculating mortgage payments?

A. $P \times (r(1+r)^n) / ((1+r)^n-1)$

B. $P \times r \times n$

C. $P / r \times n$

D. $P \times n / r$

Answer: A

The formula for calculating mortgage payments is $P \times (r(1+r)^n) / ((1+r)^n-1)$.

➡5. What is the formula for calculating the capitalization rate?

A. Net Operating Income / Current Market Value

B. Current Market Value / Net Operating Income

C. Net Operating Income $\times$ Current Market Value

D. Current Market Value $\times$ Net Operating Income

Answer: A

The capitalization rate is calculated as Net Operating Income divided by Current Market Value.

➡6. What does CMA stand for in real estate calculations?

A. Comparative Market Analysis

B. Capital Market Assessment

C. Current Market Appraisal

D. Comparative Monetary Assessment

Answer: A

CMA stands for Comparative Market Analysis, used for property valuation.

➡7. What is the formula for calculating Cash-on-Cash Return?

A. Annual Cash Flow / Total Cash Invested × 100

B. Total Cash Invested / Annual Cash Flow × 100

C. Annual Cash Flow × Total Cash Invested

D. Total Cash Invested × Annual Cash Flow

Answer: A

Cash-on-Cash Return is calculated as Annual Cash Flow divided by Total Cash Invested, multiplied by 100.

➡8. What is the formula for calculating prorations?

A. Annual Cost / 365 × Number of Days

B. Annual Cost × 365 / Number of Days

C. Number of Days / Annual Cost × 365

D. Number of Days × Annual Cost / 365

Answer: A

Prorations are calculated as Annual Cost divided by 365, multiplied by the Number of Days.

➡9. What is the formula for calculating cubic footage?

A. Length × Width × Height

B. Length × Width

C. Length × Height

D. Width × Height

Answer: A

Cubic footage is calculated by multiplying the length, width, and height of the space.

➡10. What is the formula for calculating commissions?

192

A. Sale Price × Commission Rate

B. Commission Rate × Sale Price

C. Sale Price / Commission Rate

D. Commission Rate / Sale Price

Answer: A

Commissions are calculated as Sale Price multiplied by Commission Rate.

➠11. **What is the formula for calculating Gross Rent Multiplier (GRM)?**

A. Property Price / Gross Annual Rents

B. Gross Annual Rents / Property Price

C. Property Price × Gross Annual Rents

D. Gross Annual Rents × Property Price

Answer: A

The Gross Rent Multiplier (GRM) is calculated by dividing the property price by the gross annual rents.

➠12. **What is the formula for calculating depreciation?**

A. (Cost of the Property - Salvage Value) / Useful Life

B. (Salvage Value - Cost of the Property) / Useful Life

C. Cost of the Property × Salvage Value

D. Salvage Value × Cost of the Property

Answer: A

Depreciation is calculated by subtracting the salvage value from the cost of the property and dividing by its useful life.

➠13. **What does PITI stand for in mortgage calculations?**

A. Principal, Interest, Taxes, Insurance

B. Payment, Interest, Taxes, Insurance

C. Principal, Income, Taxes, Insurance

D. Payment, Income, Taxes, Insurance

Answer: A

PITI stands for Principal, Interest, Taxes, and Insurance, which are the four components of a mortgage payment.

➡14. What is the formula for calculating equity?

A. Market Value - Mortgage Balance

B. Mortgage Balance - Market Value

C. Market Value × Mortgage Balance

D. Mortgage Balance × Market Value

Answer: A

Equity is calculated as the market value of the property minus the mortgage balance.

➡15. What is the formula for calculating net operating income (NOI)?

A. Gross Income - Operating Expenses

B. Operating Expenses - Gross Income

C. Gross Income × Operating Expenses

D. Operating Expenses × Gross Income

Answer: A

Net Operating Income (NOI) is calculated by subtracting operating expenses from gross income.

➡16. What is the formula for calculating the break-even point?

A. Fixed Costs / (Selling Price - Variable Costs)

B. (Selling Price - Variable Costs) / Fixed Costs

C. Fixed Costs × (Selling Price - Variable Costs)

D. (Selling Price - Variable Costs) × Fixed Costs

Answer: A

The break-even point is calculated by dividing fixed costs by the difference between the selling price and variable costs.

➡17. What is the formula for calculating the internal rate of return (IRR)?

A. NPV = 0

B. ROI = 100%

C. NPV × ROI

D. ROI × NPV

Answer: A

The internal rate of return (IRR) is the discount rate that makes the net present value (NPV) of all cash flows equal to zero.

➡18. What is the formula for calculating the price per square foot?

A. Total Price / Total Square Footage

B. Total Square Footage / Total Price

C. Total Price × Total Square Footage

D. Total Square Footage × Total Price

Answer: A.

The price per square foot is calculated by dividing the total price by the total square footage.

➡19. What is the formula for calculating the amortization schedule?

A. $P \times (r(1+r)^n) / ((1+r)^n - 1)$

B. P × r × n

C. P / r × n

D. P × n / r

Answer: A

The formula for calculating the amortization schedule is P × (r(1+r)^n) / ((1+r)^n-1).

→20. What is the formula for calculating the future value of an investment?

A. P × (1 + r)^n

B. P × (1 - r)^n

C. P / (1 + r)^n

D. P / (1 - r)^n

Answer: A

The future value of an investment is calculated as P × (1 + r)^n.

→21. How do you calculate the Net Operating Income (NOI) for a property?

A. Gross Income - Operating Expenses

B. Gross Income + Operating Expenses

C. Operating Expenses - Gross Income

D. Gross Income × Operating Expenses

Answer: A

Net Operating Income is calculated by subtracting the operating expenses from the gross income.

→22. What is the formula for calculating the loan-to-value ratio (LTV)?

A. Mortgage Amount / Appraised Value

B. Appraised Value / Mortgage Amount

C. Mortgage Amount × Appraised Value

D. Appraised Value × Mortgage Amount

Answer: A

The loan-to-value ratio (LTV) is calculated by dividing the mortgage amount by the appraised value of the property.

➡ **23. What is the formula for calculating the cash-on-cash return?**

A. Annual Pre-tax Cash Flow / Total Cash Invested

B. Total Cash Invested / Annual Pre-tax Cash Flow

C. Annual Pre-tax Cash Flow × Total Cash Invested

D. Total Cash Invested × Annual Pre-tax Cash Flow

Answer: A

The cash-on-cash return is calculated by dividing the annual pre-tax cash flow by the total cash invested.

➡ **24. What is the formula for calculating the debt service coverage ratio (DSCR)?**

A. Net Operating Income / Debt Service

B. Debt Service / Net Operating Income

C. Net Operating Income × Debt Service

D. Debt Service × Net Operating Income

Answer: A

The debt service coverage ratio (DSCR) is calculated by dividing the net operating income by the debt service.

➡ **25. What is the formula for calculating the equity build-up rate?**

A. (Principal Paid in Year 1 / Initial Investment) × 100

B. (Initial Investment / Principal Paid in Year 1) × 100

C. Principal Paid in Year 1 × Initial Investment

D. Initial Investment × Principal Paid in Year 1

Answer: A

The equity build-up rate is calculated by dividing the principal paid in the first year by the initial investment and then multiplying by 100.

➡26. What is the formula for calculating the gross operating income (GOI)?

A. Gross Potential Income - Vacancy and Credit Losses

B. Vacancy and Credit Losses - Gross Potential Income

C. Gross Potential Income × Vacancy and Credit Losses

D. Vacancy and Credit Losses × Gross Potential Income

Answer: A

The gross operating income (GOI) is calculated by subtracting vacancy and credit losses from the gross potential income.

➡27. What is the formula for calculating the effective gross income (EGI)?

A. Gross Operating Income + Other Income

B. Other Income - Gross Operating Income

C. Gross Operating Income × Other Income

D. Other Income × Gross Operating Income

Answer: A

The effective gross income (EGI) is calculated by adding other income to the gross operating income.

➡28. What is the formula for calculating the absorption rate?

A. Number of Units Sold / Number of Units Available

B. Number of Units Available / Number of Units Sold

C. Number of Units Sold × Number of Units Available

D. Number of Units Available × Number of Units Sold

Answer: A

The absorption rate is calculated by dividing the number of units sold by the number of units available.

➡ **29. What is the formula for calculating the price-to-rent ratio?**

A. Home Price / Annual Rent

B. Annual Rent / Home Price

C. Home Price × Annual Rent

D. Annual Rent × Home Price

Answer: A

The price-to-rent ratio is calculated by dividing the home price by the annual rent.

➡ **30. What is the formula for calculating the yield?**

A. Annual Income / Investment Cost

B. Investment Cost / Annual Income

C. Annual Income × Investment Cost

D. Investment Cost × Annual Income

Answer: A

The yield is calculated by dividing the annual income by the investment cost.

➡ **31. What is the formula for calculating the Gross Rent Multiplier (GRM)?**

A. Sales Price / Monthly Rent

B. Monthly Rent / Sales Price

C. Sales Price × Monthly Rent

D. Monthly Rent × Sales Price

Answer: A

The Gross Rent Multiplier (GRM) is calculated by dividing the sales price by the monthly rent.

→32. **How do you calculate the Loan-to-Value ratio (LTV)?**

A. Loan Amount / Appraised Value

B. Appraised Value / Loan Amount

C. Loan Amount × Appraised Value

D. Appraised Value × Loan Amount

Answer: A

The Loan-to-Value ratio (LTV) is calculated by dividing the loan amount by the appraised value of the property.

→33. **How do you calculate the Net Operating Income (NOI)?**

A. Gross Operating Income - Operating Expenses

B. Operating Expenses - Gross Operating Income

C. Gross Operating Income × Operating Expenses

D. Operating Expenses × Gross Operating Income

Answer: A

The Net Operating Income (NOI) is calculated by subtracting the operating expenses from the gross operating income.

→34. **How do you calculate the Debt Service Coverage Ratio (DSCR)?**

A. Net Operating Income / Debt Service

B. Debt Service / Net Operating Income

C. Net Operating Income × Debt Service

D. Debt Service × Net Operating Income

Answer: A

The Debt Service Coverage Ratio (DSCR) is calculated by dividing the Net Operating Income by the Debt Service.

➡35. What is the formula for calculating the Break-Even Ratio (BER)?

A. (Operating Expenses + Debt Service) / Gross Operating Income

B. Gross Operating Income / (Operating Expenses + Debt Service)

C. (Operating Expenses + Debt Service) × Gross Operating Income

D. Gross Operating Income × (Operating Expenses + Debt Service)

Answer: A

The Break-Even Ratio (BER) is calculated by dividing the sum of operating expenses and debt service by the gross operating income.

➡36. How do you calculate the Effective Gross Income (EGI)?

A. Gross Income - Vacancy Losses + Other Income

B. Gross Income + Vacancy Losses - Other Income

C. Gross Income × Vacancy Losses + Other Income

D. Gross Income + Vacancy Losses × Other Income

Answer: A

The Effective Gross Income (EGI) is calculated by subtracting vacancy losses from the gross income and adding any other income.

➡37. What is the formula for calculating the Operating Expense Ratio (OER)?

A. Operating Expenses / Effective Gross Income

B. Effective Gross Income / Operating Expenses

C. Operating Expenses × Effective Gross Income

D. Effective Gross Income × Operating Expenses

Answer: A

The Operating Expense Ratio (OER) is calculated by dividing the operating expenses by the effective gross income.

➡38. How do you calculate the Cash-on-Cash Return?

A. Cash Flow Before Taxes / Initial Investment

B. Initial Investment / Cash Flow Before Taxes

C. Cash Flow Before Taxes × Initial Investment

D. Initial Investment × Cash Flow Before Taxes

Answer: A

The Cash-on-Cash Return is calculated by dividing the cash flow before taxes by the initial investment.

➡39. What is the formula for calculating the Amortization Factor?

A. Monthly Payment / Loan Amount

B. Loan Amount / Monthly Payment

C. Monthly Payment × Loan Amount

D. Loan Amount × Monthly Payment

Answer: A

The Amortization Factor is calculated by dividing the monthly payment by the loan amount.

➡40. How do you calculate the Equity Dividend Rate (EDR)?

A. Cash Flow After Taxes / Equity Investment

B. Equity Investment / Cash Flow After Taxes

C. Cash Flow After Taxes × Equity Investment

D. Equity Investment × Cash Flow After Taxes

➡ **41. What is the formula for calculating the Debt Service Coverage Ratio (DSCR)?**

A. Net Operating Income / Debt Service

B. Debt Service / Net Operating Income

C. Net Operating Income × Debt Service

D. Debt Service - Net Operating Income

Answer: A

The Debt Service Coverage Ratio is calculated by dividing the Net Operating Income by the Debt Service.

➡ **42. How do you calculate the Gross Rent Multiplier (GRM)?**

A. Property Price / Monthly Rent

B. Monthly Rent / Property Price

C. Annual Rent / Property Price

D. Property Price / Annual Rent

Answer: A

The Gross Rent Multiplier is calculated by dividing the property price by the monthly rent.

➡ **43. What is the formula for calculating Loan-to-Value ratio?**

A. Loan Amount / Property Value

B. Property Value / Loan Amount

C. Loan Amount × Property Value

D. Property Value - Loan Amount

Answer: A

The Loan-to-Value ratio is calculated by dividing the loan amount by the property value.

➡️**44. How do you calculate the break-even point in a real estate investment?**

    A. Fixed Costs / (Selling Price - Variable Costs)

    B. (Selling Price - Variable Costs) / Fixed Costs

    C. Fixed Costs × Selling Price

    D. Selling Price / Fixed Costs

Answer: A

The break-even point is calculated by dividing the fixed costs by the difference between the selling price and variable costs.

➡️**45. How do you calculate the Return on Investment (ROI) for a property?**

    A. (Net Profit / Investment Cost) × 100

    B. (Investment Cost / Net Profit) × 100

    C. Net Profit × Investment Cost

    D. Investment Cost - Net Profit

Answer: A

The Return on Investment is calculated by dividing the net profit by the investment cost and then multiplying by 100.

➡️**46. How do you calculate the equity in a property?**

    A. Property Value - Mortgage Balance

    B. Mortgage Balance - Property Value

    C. Property Value × Mortgage Balance

    D. Mortgage Balance / Property Value

Answer: A

Equity is calculated by subtracting the mortgage balance from the property value.

➡️**47. What is the formula for calculating the amortization payment?**

    A. Principal Amount / Number of Payments

    B. Interest Rate / Number of Payments

    C. (Principal Amount × Interest Rate) / Number of Payments

    D. (Principal Amount × Interest Rate) / (1 - (1 + Interest Rate)^-Number of Payments)

Answer: D

The amortization payment is calculated using the formula mentioned.

➡️**48. What is the formula for calculating the Internal Rate of Return (IRR) for a real estate investment?**

    A. The discount rate that makes the Net Present Value zero

    B. The rate that equals the Net Operating Income

    C. The rate that equals the Debt Service

    D. The rate that makes the Gross Income zero

Answer: A

The Internal Rate of Return is the discount rate that makes the Net Present Value of all cash flows from a particular investment equal to zero.

➡️**49. What is the formula for calculating the rate of return on an investment property?**

    A. (Net Profit / Cost of Investment) × 100

    B. (Cost of Investment / Net Profit) × 100

    C. Net Profit × Cost of Investment

D. Cost of Investment - Net Profit

Answer: A

The rate of return is calculated by dividing the net profit by the cost of the investment and then multiplying by 100.

➡50. How do you calculate the net profit from a real estate investment?

A. Selling Price - (Buying Price + Costs)

B. (Buying Price + Costs) - Selling Price

C. Selling Price × Buying Price

D. Buying Price / Selling Price

Answer: A

The Net Operating Income (NOI) is calculated by subtracting the operating expenses from the gross operating income.

Specialty Areas

The real estate industry is a vast and multifaceted field, offering a range of specialty areas for professionals to focus on. Whether you're interested in residential, commercial, or investment properties, there's a niche for everyone. This chapter will explore the various specialty areas within the Illinois real estate market, providing insights into each sector's unique characteristics, challenges, and opportunities.

- **Residential Real Estate**

Single-Family Homes

Single-family homes are the most common type of residential real estate. They offer privacy and are generally more spacious, making them ideal for families.

Condominiums

Condominiums are multi-unit buildings where each unit is owned individually. They are popular in urban areas and often come with amenities like gyms and swimming pools.

Townhouses

Townhouses are multi-floor homes that share one or two walls with adjacent properties. They offer a middle ground between single-family homes and condos.

Vacation Homes

These are secondary residences often used for leisure purposes. In Illinois, areas near Lake Michigan are popular for vacation homes.

- Commercial Real Estate

Office Spaces

Office real estate can range from small, single-tenant buildings to large skyscrapers. Location and accessibility are crucial factors in determining value.

Retail Spaces

Retail spaces can be standalone shops, shopping malls, or part of a mixed-use development. The success of retail real estate often depends on consumer traffic.

Industrial Properties

These include warehouses, factories, and distribution centers. They are generally located in industrial zones and require significant investment in infrastructure.

Hotels and Hospitality

This sector includes hotels, motels, and other short-term accommodation facilities. The success of these properties often depends on location and the quality of service.

- Investment Real Estate

Rental Properties

Owning rental properties can provide a steady income stream. However, it also comes with the responsibilities of property management.

Real Estate Investment Trusts (REITs)

REITs are companies that own or finance income-producing real estate across various sectors. They offer a way to invest in real estate without owning physical property.

Flipping Properties

This involves buying properties at a low price, renovating them, and selling them at a higher price. It's a high-risk, high-reward strategy.

- Agricultural and Rural Real Estate

Farmland

Illinois is known for its fertile farmland, making agricultural real estate a viable investment. The value of farmland is determined by soil quality, location, and crop yield.

Ranches

Ranches are large pieces of land used for raising livestock. They require significant investment in facilities and equipment.

Timberland

This involves land used for logging and timber production. It's a long-term investment that requires knowledge of forestry management.

- Specialized Real Estate Services

Property Management

Property managers take care of the day-to-day operations of a property, from maintenance to tenant relations.

Real Estate Appraisal

Appraisers determine the market value of a property based on various factors like location, condition, and comparable sales.

Real Estate Consulting

Consultants offer specialized advice on property investment, market analysis, and development strategies.

- Regulatory Considerations

Each specialty area has its own set of regulations and licensing requirements. For example, commercial real estate agents may need additional certifications compared to residential agents.

- Conclusion

The Illinois real estate market offers a plethora of specialty areas for professionals to explore. Each sector comes with its own set of challenges and opportunities, making it essential for aspiring real estate agents to find their niche. Whether you're interested in residential, commercial, or investment properties, understanding the unique aspects of each specialty area will equip you with the knowledge and skills needed to succeed in this dynamic industry.

Mock Exam Specialty Areas

→1. Which type of real estate is often the entry point for many new agents and brokers?

A. Commercial

B. Industrial

C. Residential

D. Luxury

Answer: C. Residential

Explanation: The chapter states that residential real estate is often the entry point for many new agents and brokers.

→2. What type of property is a penthouse?

A. Industrial

B. Commercial

C. Residential

D. Luxury

Answer: D. Luxury

Explanation: Penthouses are high-end apartments located on the top floors of high-rise buildings and fall under luxury real estate.

→3. What is a key skill required in commercial real estate?

A. Financial Analysis

B. Knowledge of Industrial Machinery

C. Strong Interpersonal Skills

D. Discretion and Confidentiality

Answer: A. Financial Analysis

Explanation: Financial analysis is crucial in commercial real estate for understanding balance sheets, income statements, and cash flow.

➠4. What type of property is a factory?

A. Commercial

B. Industrial

C. Residential

D. Luxury

Answer: B. Industrial

Explanation: Factories are geared towards manufacturing, production, and distribution, which falls under industrial real estate.

➠5. What is a key regulatory aspect in industrial real estate?

A. Luxury tax implications

B. OSHA regulations

C. Fair Housing Laws

D. Commercial zoning laws

Answer: B. OSHA regulations

Explanation: Occupational Safety and Health Administration (OSHA) regulations are key in industrial real estate.

➠6. What type of property is a shopping mall?

A. Commercial

B. Industrial

C. Residential

D. Luxury

Answer: A. Commercial

Explanation: Shopping malls fall under commercial real estate as they are used for business activities.

➡7. What is a key skill required in luxury real estate?

A. Financial Analysis

B. Knowledge of Industrial Machinery

C. Strong Interpersonal Skills

D. Discretion and Confidentiality

Answer: D. Discretion and Confidentiality

Explanation: Clients in the luxury sector value their privacy highly, making discretion and confidentiality key skills.

➡8. What type of property is a townhouse?

A. Commercial

B. Industrial

C. Residential

D. Luxury

Answer: C. Residential

Explanation: Townhouses are multi-floor homes designed for individual or family living, which falls under residential real estate.

➡9. What is a key regulatory aspect in residential real estate?

A. Luxury tax implications

B. OSHA regulations

C. Fair Housing Laws

D. Commercial zoning laws

Answer: C. Fair Housing Laws

Explanation: Fair Housing Laws are key regulatory aspects in residential real estate to ensure equal opportunity in housing.

➡10. **What type of property is a distribution center?**

A. Commercial

B. Industrial

C. Residential

D. Luxury

Answer: B. Industrial

Explanation: Distribution centers are used for storing and distributing goods, which falls under industrial real estate.

➡11. **What type of real estate involves the sale of businesses?**

A. Commercial

B. Business Brokerage

C. Residential

D. Luxury

Answer: B. Business Brokerage

Explanation: Business Brokerage involves the sale of businesses, including their assets and real estate.

➡12. **What is a key skill required in business brokerage?**

A. Negotiation Skills

B. Knowledge of Industrial Machinery

C. Strong Interpersonal Skills

D. Financial Analysis

Answer: A. Negotiation Skills

Explanation: Negotiation skills are crucial in business brokerage to secure the best deals for clients.

➠**13. What type of real estate involves the sale of farmland?**

A. Commercial

B. Industrial

C. Agricultural

D. Luxury

Answer: C. Agricultural

Explanation: Agricultural real estate involves the sale of farmland and agricultural facilities.

➠**14. What is a key regulatory aspect in agricultural real estate?**

A. EPA Regulations

B. OSHA regulations

C. Fair Housing Laws

D. Luxury tax implications

Answer: A. EPA Regulations

Explanation: Environmental Protection Agency (EPA) regulations are key in agricultural real estate.

→15. What type of property is a hotel?

A. Commercial

B. Industrial

C. Residential

D. Hospitality

Answer: D. Hospitality

Explanation: Hotels fall under hospitality real estate, which is a sub-category of commercial real estate.

→16. What is a key skill required in hospitality real estate?

A. Customer Service

B. Knowledge of Industrial Machinery

C. Strong Interpersonal Skills

D. Financial Analysis

Answer: A. Customer Service

Explanation: Customer service is crucial in hospitality real estate to ensure guest satisfaction.

→17. What type of real estate involves the sale of undeveloped land?

A. Commercial

B. Land

C. Residential

D. Luxury

Answer: B. Land

Explanation: The sale of undeveloped land falls under land real estate.

→18. What is a key regulatory aspect in land real estate?

A. Zoning Laws

B. OSHA regulations

C. Fair Housing Laws

D. Luxury tax implications

Answer: A. Zoning Laws

Explanation: Zoning laws are key in land real estate to determine the types of development that can occur.

➡19. What type of property is a condominium?

A. Commercial

B. Industrial

C. Residential

D. Luxury

Answer: C. Residential

Explanation: Condominiums are multi-unit properties that are sold individually, which falls under residential real estate.

➡20. What is a key skill required in land real estate?

A. Negotiation Skills

B. Knowledge of Zoning Laws

C. Strong Interpersonal Skills

D. Financial Analysis

Answer: B. Knowledge of Zoning Laws

Explanation: Knowledge of zoning laws is crucial in land real estate to guide clients on permissible uses.

➡21. What is the primary focus of industrial real estate?

A. Warehouses

B. Hotels

C. Farmland

D. Condominiums

Answer: A. Warehouses

Explanation: Industrial real estate primarily focuses on warehouses and manufacturing buildings.

➡22. What is a 1031 exchange commonly used for?

A. Residential properties

B. Commercial properties

C. Agricultural properties

D. Industrial properties

Answer: B. Commercial properties

Explanation: A 1031 exchange is commonly used to defer capital gains tax in commercial real estate.

➡23. What is the main consideration in retail real estate?

A. Location

B. Size

C. Zoning

D. Tax implications

Answer: A. Location

Explanation: Location is the main consideration in retail real estate, as it directly impacts customer footfall.

➡24. What is the primary focus of residential real estate?

A. Single-family homes

B. Warehouses

C. Hotels

D. Farmland

Answer: **A. Single-family homes**

Explanation: Residential real estate primarily focuses on single-family homes, although it can include multi-family units.

➡25. What is the main consideration in luxury real estate?

A. Price

B. Location

C. Amenities

D. Size

Answer: **C. Amenities**

Explanation: Luxury real estate often focuses on the amenities offered, such as pools, gyms, and concierge services.

➡26. What is the primary advantage of investing in mixed-use real estate?

A. Diversification

B. Lower taxes

C. Easier management

D. Higher rent

Answer: **A. Diversification**

Explanation: Mixed-use real estate offers diversification as it combines residential, commercial, and sometimes industrial spaces.

→27. What is the main disadvantage of investing in vacation real estate?

A. Seasonal income

B. High maintenance

C. Zoning restrictions

D. High taxes

Answer: **A. Seasonal income**

Explanation: Vacation real estate often has seasonal income, which can be a disadvantage for consistent cash flow.

→28. What is the primary consideration when investing in student housing?

A. Proximity to educational institutions

B. Luxury amenities

C. Tax benefits

D. Size of the property

Answer: **A. Proximity to educational institutions**

Explanation: The primary consideration for student housing is its proximity to educational institutions.

→29. What is the main benefit of investing in senior living communities?

A. Lower maintenance

B. Steady income

C. Tax benefits

D. High rent

Answer: **B. Steady income**

Explanation: Senior living communities often provide a steady income due to long-term leases.

➡ **30. What is a triple net lease commonly used in?**

A. Residential properties

B. Commercial properties

C. Industrial properties

D. Agricultural properties

Answer: B. Commercial properties

Explanation: A triple net lease is commonly used in commercial real estate, where the tenant pays property taxes, insurance, and maintenance costs.

➡ **31. What is the primary focus of hospitality real estate?**

A. Hotels and resorts

B. Warehouses

C. Office buildings

D. Farmland

Answer: A. Hotels and resorts

Explanation: Hospitality real estate primarily focuses on hotels, resorts, and other lodging options.

➡ **32. What is the main consideration in agricultural real estate?**

A. Soil quality

B. Location

C. Size

D. Zoning

Answer: A. Soil quality

Explanation: Soil quality is the main consideration in agricultural real estate for farming purposes.

➡33. What is the primary advantage of investing in REITs?

A. Liquidity

B. Control over property

C. Tax benefits

D. High rent

Answer: **A. Liquidity**

Explanation: REITs offer liquidity as they can be easily bought and sold on stock exchanges.

➡34. What is the main disadvantage of investing in office real estate?

A. High vacancy rates

B. Seasonal income

C. Zoning restrictions

D. High maintenance

Answer: **A. High vacancy rates**

Explanation: Office real estate can have high vacancy rates, especially in economic downturns.

➡35. What is the primary focus of mobile home parks?

A. Affordable housing

B. Luxury living

C. Commercial spaces

D. Agricultural land

Answer: **A. Affordable housing**

Explanation: Mobile home parks primarily focus on providing affordable housing options.

➡️36. What is the primary consideration when investing in retail real estate?

A. Foot traffic

B. Tax benefits

C. Size of the property

D. Proximity to educational institutions

Answer: A. Foot traffic

Explanation: Foot traffic is crucial for the success of retail real estate.

➡️37. What is the main benefit of investing in industrial real estate?

A. High rent

B. Long-term leases

C. Seasonal income

D. Tax benefits

Answer: B. Long-term leases

Explanation: Industrial real estate often comes with long-term leases, providing stable income.

➡️38. What is a common disadvantage of investing in multi-family properties?

A. High maintenance costs

B. Low rent

C. Zoning restrictions

D. Seasonal income

Answer: A. High maintenance costs

Explanation: Multi-family properties often have higher maintenance costs due to multiple units.

➡39. What is the primary focus of medical real estate?

A. Hospitals and clinics

B. Office buildings

C. Warehouses

D. Hotels and resorts

Answer: A. Hospitals and clinics

Explanation: Medical real estate primarily focuses on hospitals, clinics, and other healthcare facilities.

➡40. What is the main consideration in raw land investment?

A. Zoning restrictions

B. Soil quality

C. Location

D. Size

Answer: C. Location

Explanation: Location is key in raw land investment for future development.

➡41. What is the primary advantage of investing in storage units?

A. Low maintenance

B. High rent

C. Tax benefits

D. Seasonal income

Answer: A. Low maintenance

Explanation: Storage units generally require low maintenance.

➡42. What is the main disadvantage of investing in co-working spaces?

A. High vacancy rates

B. Low rent

C. Zoning restrictions

D. Seasonal income

Answer: A. High vacancy rates

Explanation: Co-working spaces can have high vacancy rates, especially during economic downturns.

➡43. What is the primary focus of green real estate?

A. Energy efficiency

B. High rent

C. Tax benefits

D. Size of the property

Answer: A. Energy efficiency

Explanation: Green real estate primarily focuses on energy-efficient buildings.

➡44. What is the main benefit of investing in brownfield sites?

A. Tax incentives

B. High rent

C. Seasonal income

D. Long-term leases

Answer: A. Tax incentives

Explanation: Brownfield sites often come with tax incentives for redevelopment.

➡ **45. What is the primary consideration when investing in infill real estate?**

A. Location

B. Size

C. Zoning restrictions

D. Soil quality

Answer: A. Location

Explanation: Infill real estate focuses on developing vacant or underused parcels within existing urban areas, so location is key.

➡ **46. What is the main disadvantage of investing in luxury real estate?**

A. High maintenance costs

B. Seasonal income

C. Zoning restrictions

D. Low rent

Answer: A. High maintenance costs

Explanation: Luxury real estate often comes with high maintenance costs.

➡ **47. What is the primary focus of transit-oriented development?**

A. Proximity to public transport

B. Luxury amenities

C. Tax benefits

D. Size of the property

Answer: A. Proximity to public transport

Explanation: Transit-oriented development focuses on properties close to public transport facilities.

➡48. What is the main benefit of investing in adaptive reuse properties?

A. Tax incentives

B. High rent

C. Seasonal income

D. Long-term leases

Answer: A. Tax incentives

Explanation: Adaptive reuse properties often come with tax incentives for redevelopment.

➡49. What is the primary consideration when investing in distressed properties?

A. Cost of renovation

B. Location

C. Size

D. Zoning

Answer: A. Cost of renovation

Explanation: The cost of renovation is a key consideration when investing in distressed properties.

➡50. What is the main disadvantage of investing in fixer-uppers?

A. High renovation costs

B. Low rent

C. Zoning restrictions

D. Seasonal income

Answer: A. High renovation costs

Explanation: Fixer-uppers often come with high renovation costs that can eat into profits.

Ethics and Legal Considerations

Ethics and legal considerations are the backbone of any profession, and real estate is no exception. In Illinois, real estate professionals are bound by both state laws and industry ethics to ensure fair and transparent transactions. This chapter delves into the ethical and legal considerations that every real estate professional in Illinois should be aware of.

- Ethical Considerations

Code of Ethics

The National Association of Realtors (NAR) provides a Code of Ethics that serves as a guide for real estate professionals. It covers duties to clients, the public, and other realtors, emphasizing honesty, integrity, and professionalism.

Fiduciary Duty

Real estate agents have a fiduciary duty to their clients, meaning they must act in the best interest of their clients at all times. This includes confidentiality, full disclosure, and loyalty.

Dual Agency

Dual agency occurs when a real estate agent represents both the buyer and the seller in a transaction. While legal in Illinois, it poses ethical challenges and requires informed consent from all parties.

Misrepresentation and Fraud

Deliberately providing false information or concealing material facts is not only unethical but also illegal. Agents must be transparent and honest in all dealings.

- Legal Considerations

Licensing Requirements

In Illinois, real estate professionals must be licensed by the Illinois Department of Financial and Professional Regulation (IDFPR). The requirements include education, examination, and ongoing professional development.

Fair Housing Laws

The Fair Housing Act prohibits discrimination based on race, color, religion, sex, or national origin. Illinois state laws further extend these protections to include sexual orientation and marital status.

Disclosure Requirements

Illinois law requires sellers to provide a Residential Real Property Disclosure Report, detailing the condition of the property. Failure to disclose known issues can result in legal consequences.

Contract Laws

Real estate contracts in Illinois must be in writing to be enforceable. They should clearly outline the terms and conditions, including price, closing date, and contingencies.

Zoning and Land Use Laws

Illinois has specific zoning laws that dictate how a property can be used. Violating these laws can result in fines and legal action.

- Risk Management

Professional Liability Insurance

Also known as Errors and Omissions (E&O) insurance, this protects real estate professionals against legal claims for mistakes or negligence in their services.

Record-Keeping

Maintaining accurate and complete records of all transactions is not only good practice but also a legal requirement. These records can be crucial in resolving disputes or legal claims.

Continuing Education

Illinois requires real estate professionals to complete continuing education to renew their licenses. This ensures they stay updated on legal changes and ethical guidelines.

- Case Studies

Case Study 1: Fair Housing Violation

An Illinois real estate agent was found guilty of steering minority clients away from predominantly white neighborhoods. This is a violation of both NAR's Code of Ethics and federal Fair Housing laws.

Case Study 2: Breach of Fiduciary Duty

An agent in Illinois was sued for failing to disclose a property's flooding history. The court ruled in favor of the client, citing a breach of fiduciary duty and lack of full disclosure.

- Conclusion

Ethics and legal considerations are integral to the practice of real estate in Illinois. Understanding and adhering to ethical guidelines and state laws not only enhances your reputation but also minimizes legal risks. From fiduciary duties to fair housing laws, a strong ethical foundation is essential for anyone looking to succeed in the Illinois real estate market.

Mock Exam Ethics and Legal Considerations

➡1. What are the three main categories of the NAR Code of Ethics?

A. Duties to Clients, Duties to Realtors, Duties to the Public

B. Duties to Clients and Customers, Duties to the Public, Duties to Realtors

C. Duties to Sellers, Duties to Buyers, Duties to the Public

D. Duties to the Government, Duties to Clients, Duties to Realtors

Answer: B

The NAR Code of Ethics is divided into three main categories: Duties to Clients and Customers, Duties to the Public, and Duties to Realtors.

➡2. Which of the following is NOT a fiduciary duty?

A. Loyalty

B. Confidentiality

C. Manipulation

D. Full Disclosure

Answer: C

Manipulation is not a fiduciary duty. The fiduciary duties are loyalty, confidentiality, obedience, reasonable care, accounting, and full disclosure.

➡3. What is the primary purpose of zoning laws?

A. To increase property taxes

B. To regulate land use

C. To protect endangered species

D. To promote business

Answer: B

The primary purpose of zoning laws is to regulate land use, such as residential, commercial, or industrial zones.

➡4. What does 'reasonable care' in fiduciary duties imply?

A. Taking vacations regularly

B. Staying updated on market trends

C. Investing in real estate

D. Focusing on commission

Answer: B

'Reasonable care' means staying updated on market trends, legal changes, and other factors that could affect a client's decision.

➡5. What is the consequence of not adhering to full disclosure?

A. Increased commission

B. Legal repercussions

C. More clients

D. Promotion

Answer: B

Failing to adhere to full disclosure can lead to legal repercussions, including lawsuits and loss of license.

➡6. Which federal law is designed to ensure fair housing?

A. The Sherman Act

B. The Fair Housing Act

C. The Clayton Act

D. The Dodd-Frank Act

Answer: B

The Fair Housing Act is designed to prevent discrimination in housing based on race, color, religion, sex, or national origin.

➡7. What is the minimum age requirement for obtaining a real estate license in most states?

A. 16

B. 18

C. 21

D. 25

Answer: B

The minimum age requirement for obtaining a real estate license in most states is 18 years.

➡8. What is the key to resolving ethical dilemmas like dual agency?

A. Ignoring the issue

B. Full disclosure and informed consent

C. Choosing one party to represent

D. Consulting a lawyer

Answer: B

The key to resolving ethical dilemmas like dual agency lies in full disclosure and obtaining informed consent from all parties involved.

➡9. Which of the following is NOT an element that makes a contract legally binding?

A. Offer and acceptance

B. Consideration

C. Coercion

D. Legality of purpose

Answer: C

Coercion is not an element that makes a contract legally binding. A contract must have offer and acceptance, consideration, and legality of purpose to be legally binding.

➠**10. What does the NAR Code of Ethics say about advertising?**

A. It encourages aggressive advertising

B. It prohibits all forms of advertising

C. It requires truthful advertising

D. It promotes online advertising only

Answer: C

The NAR Code of Ethics requires that all advertising be truthful and not misleading.

➠**11. What is the primary role of the Real Estate Commission in most states?**

A. To sell properties

B. To regulate and license real estate agents

C. To build homes

D. To provide loans

Answer: B

The primary role of the Real Estate Commission in most states is to regulate and license real estate agents.

➠**12. What is the statute of frauds?**

A. A law that requires certain contracts to be in writing

B. A law that allows fraud in certain cases

C. A law that regulates online advertising

D. A law that deals with zoning issues

Answer: A

The statute of frauds is a law that requires certain contracts, like those for the sale of real estate, to be in writing to be enforceable.

➡13. What does RESPA stand for?

A. Real Estate Settlement Procedures Act

B. Real Estate Sales Professional Act

C. Residential Sales Property Act

D. Real Estate Security Policy Act

Answer: A

RESPA stands for Real Estate Settlement Procedures Act, which aims to provide transparency in the home buying process.

➡14. What is puffing in real estate terms?

A. Illegal misrepresentation

B. Exaggeration of property features

C. Accurate description of property

D. Undervaluing a property

Answer: B

Puffing refers to the exaggeration of property features, which is generally considered legal but can be ethically questionable.

➡15. What is the primary purpose of an escrow account?

A. To hold funds for investment

B. To hold funds until the completion of a real estate transaction

C. To pay for the agent's commission

D. To pay property taxes

Answer: B

The primary purpose of an escrow account is to hold funds until the completion of a real estate transaction.

➡16. What does the term "redlining" refer to?

A. Drawing property boundaries

B. Discriminatory lending practices

C. Marking properties for demolition

D. Highlighting important clauses in a contract

Answer: B

Redlining refers to discriminatory lending practices that deny loans or insurance to people based on their location, often targeting minority communities.

➡17. What is the difference between ethics and laws?

A. Ethics are legally binding, laws are not

B. Laws are legally binding, ethics are not

C. Ethics and laws are the same

D. Laws are optional, ethics are mandatory

Answer: B

Laws are legally binding rules that must be followed, while ethics are moral principles that guide behavior but are not legally enforceable.

➡18. What is the "doctrine of caveat emptor"?

A. Let the buyer beware

B. Let the seller beware

C. Buyer's premium

D. Seller's advantage

Answer: A

The doctrine of "caveat emptor" means "let the buyer beware," indicating that the buyer is responsible for due diligence.

➡19. What is a bilateral contract?

A. A contract with only one party

B. A contract with two parties

C. A contract with multiple parties

D. A contract that is not legally binding

Answer: B

A bilateral contract is a contract involving two parties where each party has made a promise to the other.

➡20. What is the role of a title company?

A. To market properties

B. To ensure the title is clear and prepare for its transfer

C. To provide loans

D. To build homes

Answer: B

The role of a title company is to ensure that the title to a piece of real estate is legitimate and to prepare for its transfer from the seller to the buyer.

21. What is the "dual agency" in real estate?

A. When an agent represents both the buyer and the seller

B. When two agents work for the same client

C. When an agent works for two different real estate firms

D. When an agent sells both commercial and residential properties

Answer: A

Dual agency occurs when a real estate agent represents both the buyer and the seller in the same transaction.

22. What does the Fair Housing Act prohibit?

A. Discrimination based on race, color, religion, sex, or national origin

B. All forms of discrimination

C. Discrimination based on financial status

D. Discrimination based on occupation

Answer: A

The Fair Housing Act prohibits discrimination in housing based on race, color, religion, sex, or national origin.

23. What is earnest money?

A. Money paid by the buyer at the time of the property closing

B. A refundable deposit

C. Money paid by the buyer to show serious intent to purchase

D. Money paid by the seller as a part of the listing agreement

Answer: C

Earnest money is money paid by the buyer to show serious intent to purchase the property.

➡24. What is a contingency in a real estate contract?

A. A binding clause

B. A non-negotiable term

C. A condition that must be met for the contract to be binding

D. A penalty for breach of contract

Answer: C

A contingency is a condition that must be met for the contract to be binding, such as a home inspection.

➡25. What is a fiduciary duty?

A. A legal obligation to act in the best interest of another

B. A duty to find the best property for a client

C. A duty to sell a property as quickly as possible

D. A duty to maximize profit

Answer: A

A fiduciary duty is a legal obligation to act in the best interest of another, such as a client.

➡26. What is a unilateral contract?

A. A contract where only one party makes a promise

B. A contract where both parties make promises

C. A contract that involves more than two parties

D. A contract that is not legally binding

Answer: A

A unilateral contract is a contract where only one party makes a promise, and the other has the option to complete the action.

➡ 27. What is the purpose of a disclosure statement?

A. To disclose the agent's commission

B. To disclose any known defects or issues with the property

C. To disclose the buyer's financial status

D. To disclose the terms of the mortgage

Answer: B

The purpose of a disclosure statement is to disclose any known defects or issues with the property to the buyer.

➡ 28. What does "time is of the essence" mean in a real estate contract?

A. Deadlines must be strictly adhered to

B. Time limits are flexible

C. The contract has no expiration date

D. The contract can be terminated at any time

Answer: A

"Time is of the essence" means that deadlines set forth in the contract must be strictly adhered to.

➡ 29. What is a quitclaim deed?

A. A deed that transfers property with no warranties

B. A deed that includes warranties

C. A deed that transfers leasehold interest

D. A deed that can be easily revoked

Answer: A

A quitclaim deed is a deed that transfers property with no warranties or guarantees.

→30. What is the role of a notary public in a real estate transaction?

A. To negotiate the terms

B. To verify the identity of the parties and witness the signing of documents

C. To provide legal advice

D. To inspect the property

Answer: B

The role of a notary public is to verify the identity of the parties and witness the signing of important documents.

→31. What is the primary purpose of a title search?

A. To determine the property's market value

B. To verify the legal owner of the property

C. To inspect the condition of the property

D. To assess property taxes

Answer: B

The primary purpose of a title search is to verify the legal owner of the property and ensure there are no liens or other encumbrances.

→32. What is a "balloon payment" in a mortgage?

A. A small initial payment

B. A large final payment

C. A regular monthly payment

D. An extra payment to reduce interest

Answer: B

A balloon payment is a large final payment at the end of a loan term, usually after a series of smaller payments.

➡ 33. What is the "right of first refusal" in real estate?

A. The right to refuse a sale

B. The right to be the first to purchase a property before the owner sells it to another party

C. The right to refuse to pay rent

D. The right to refuse a home inspection

Answer: B

The right of first refusal allows an individual or entity the opportunity to purchase a property before the owner sells it to another party.

➡ 34. What is a "listing agreement"?

A. An agreement between buyer and seller

B. An agreement between a seller and a real estate agent

C. An agreement between a buyer and a real estate agent

D. An agreement between two real estate agents

Answer: B

A listing agreement is a contract between a seller and a real estate agent outlining the terms under which the agent will sell the property.

➡ 35. What does "under contract" mean in real estate?

A. The property is being appraised

B. The property is being inspected

C. An offer on the property has been accepted, but the sale is not yet complete

D. The property has been sold

Answer: C

"Under contract" means that an offer on the property has been accepted, but the sale is not yet complete, pending contingencies or other terms.

➡ 36. What is the role of a fiduciary in a real estate transaction?

A. To act in the best interest of the client

B. To maximize profits for the brokerage

C. To represent both buyer and seller equally

D. To ensure the property passes inspection

Answer: A

The role of a fiduciary is to act in the best interest of the client, whether that's the buyer or the seller.

➡ 37. What does "escrow" refer to in real estate?

A. A type of mortgage loan

B. A neutral third party holding funds or documents until conditions are met

C. A binding contract between buyer and seller

D. A home inspection report

Answer: B

Escrow refers to a neutral third party holding funds or documents until certain conditions are met in a real estate transaction.

➡ 38. What is a "contingency" in a real estate contract?

A. A penalty for late payment

B. A condition that must be met for the contract to proceed

C. An optional add-on to the property

D. A mandatory fee paid to the real estate agent

Answer: B

A contingency is a condition that must be met for the contract to proceed, such as a successful home inspection.

➡ **39. What does "amortization" mean in the context of a mortgage?**

A. The process of increasing the loan amount

B. The process of paying off the loan over time

C. The process of adjusting the interest rate

D. The process of transferring the loan to another lender

Answer: B

Amortization is the process of paying off a loan over time through regular payments.

➡ **40. What is "due diligence" in real estate?**

A. The responsibility to investigate a property before purchase

B. The obligation to pay property taxes

C. The requirement to obtain a mortgage pre-approval

D. The duty to disclose all known defects to a buyer

Answer: A

Due diligence is the responsibility of the buyer to investigate a property thoroughly before completing the purchase.

➡ **41. What is "redlining" in the context of real estate?**

A. Drawing property boundaries

B. Discriminatory practice affecting mortgage availability

C. A type of home inspection

D. A negotiation strategy

Answer: B

Redlining is a discriminatory practice where mortgage lenders deny loans or insurance to certain areas based on racial or ethnic composition.

➡️**42. What does "title insurance" protect against?**

A. Property damage

B. Mortgage default

C. Legal claims against property ownership

D. Loss of rental income

Answer: C

Title insurance protects against legal claims challenging the ownership of the property.

➡️**43. What is "dual agency" in real estate?**

A. When an agent represents both the buyer and the seller

B. When two agents from the same brokerage represent the buyer and the seller

C. When an agent represents two buyers for the same property

D. When an agent represents two sellers for different properties

Answer: A

Dual agency occurs when a real estate agent represents both the buyer and the seller in the same transaction. This can create a conflict of interest and is illegal in some states.

➡️**44. What is a "balloon mortgage"?**

A. A mortgage with fluctuating interest rates

B. A mortgage that requires a large final payment

C. A mortgage with no down payment

D. A mortgage paid off in less than 5 years

Answer: B

A balloon mortgage requires a large final payment at the end of the loan term.

➡️**45. What is "blockbusting"?**

A. Building multiple properties in a short time

B. Encouraging people to sell their homes by instigating fear of a changing neighborhood

C. The process of rezoning land

D. Buying large blocks of property for development

Answer: B

Blockbusting is the practice of encouraging people to sell their homes by instigating fear, often related to racial, ethnic, or social change in a neighborhood.

➡️**46. What is a "1031 exchange"?**

A. A tax-deferred property exchange

B. A type of mortgage loan

C. A property auction

D. An open house event

Answer: A

A 1031 exchange allows the owner to sell a property and reinvest the proceeds in a new property while deferring capital gains tax.

➡️**47. What is "eminent domain"?**

A. The right of the government to acquire private property for public use

B. The highest legal ownership of property

C. A type of zoning regulation

D. A clause in a mortgage contract

Answer: A

Eminent domain is the right of the government to acquire private property for public use, usually with compensation.

➡️**48. What is "equity" in real estate?**

A. The market value of a property

B. The difference between the property's market value and the remaining mortgage balance

C. The initial down payment

D. The annual property tax

Answer: B

Equity is the difference between the market value of the property and the remaining balance on any loans secured by the property.

➡️**49. What is "escrow" in a real estate transaction?**

A. A legal arrangement where a third party holds funds or documents

B. The initial offer made by a buyer

C. The final stage of mortgage approval

D. A type of home inspection

Answer: A

Escrow is a legal arrangement in which a third party temporarily holds funds or documents until the conditions of a contract are met.

➡️**50. What is "net operating income" in real estate investment?**

A. Gross income minus operating expenses

B. Gross income plus operating expenses

C. Mortgage payments minus rental income

D. Property value minus mortgage balance

Answer: A

Net operating income is the gross income generated by a property minus the operating expenses, not including mortgage payments or taxes.

Day of the Exam

The day of the Illinois Real Estate License Exam is a pivotal moment in your journey to becoming a licensed real estate professional. It's the culmination of months, or even years, of hard work, study, and preparation. This chapter aims to provide you with a comprehensive guide on what to expect and how to navigate the day of the exam successfully.

- Pre-Exam Preparations

The Night Before

Review Key Points: Go over your notes and flashcards, focusing on key terms, formulas, and concepts.

Check Your Exam Kit: Make sure you have all the necessary items for the exam, including your ID, exam confirmation, and any allowed materials.

Rest: Aim for at least 7-8 hours of sleep to ensure you're well-rested.

Morning of the Exam

Eat a Balanced Meal: Opt for a meal that's rich in protein and low in sugar to maintain energy levels.

Dress Comfortably: Choose attire that you'll be comfortable sitting in for an extended period.

Leave Early: Aim to arrive at least 30 minutes before the exam to account for any unexpected delays.

- At the Exam Center

Check-In Process

Identification: You'll need to present a valid ID and your exam confirmation.

Security Measures: Expect to go through a security check, including metal detectors and bag checks.

Seating: You'll be directed to your designated seat.

Exam Room Etiquette

Silence: Maintain silence throughout the exam to avoid disturbing others.

Time Management: Keep an eye on the clock but don't rush. Pace yourself.

Raise Your Hand: If you have a question or need assistance, raise your hand to get the proctor's attention.

- Taking the Exam

Multiple-Choice Questions

Read Carefully: Make sure to read each question and all answer choices carefully.

Eliminate Wrong Answers: Use the process of elimination to narrow down your choices.

Flag for Review: If you're unsure about a question, flag it and come back to it later.

Calculations and Practical Questions

Use Scratch Paper: Do your calculations on scratch paper before selecting an answer.

Double-Check: Always double-check your calculations.

Apply Real-World Logic: Use your understanding of real-world scenarios to answer practical questions.

Time Management

Pacing: Divide your time by the number of questions to get an idea of how much time you can spend on each.

Review: Use any remaining time to review flagged questions and ensure you've answered all questions.

- After the Exam

Submission: Once you're done, raise your hand to have your exam collected or submit it electronically, depending on the format.

Exit Survey: Some exams include a brief survey about your test experience.

Preliminary Results: For computer-based exams, you may receive preliminary results immediately.

- What to Do If Things Go Wrong

Technical Issues: Inform the proctor immediately if you experience any technical issues.

Misconduct: Report any observed misconduct to maintain the integrity of the exam.

Health Concerns: If you feel unwell, inform the proctor. They will guide you on the next steps.

- Conclusion

The day of the Illinois Real Estate License Exam is undoubtedly stressful, but thorough preparation can make it manageable. From the night before the exam to the moment you submit your answers, each step is crucial. Remember, this exam is not just a test of knowledge, but also of composure, attention to detail, and time management. Good luck, and may your preparation and hard work pay off in the form of a successful exam day!

After the Exam: Next Steps

Congratulations on completing the Illinois Real Estate License Exam! Whether you're confident about your performance or anxious about the results, the period following the exam is crucial for various reasons. This chapter will guide you through the steps you should take after the exam, from understanding your results to planning your real estate career.

- Understanding Your Results

Preliminary Results

Instant Feedback: For computer-based exams, you may receive preliminary results immediately after the exam.
Accuracy: These results are generally accurate but are not the final word.

Official Results

Notification: You'll receive an official notification via mail or email, usually within 1-2 weeks.
Details: The notification will include your score and information on whether you've passed or failed.

Score Breakdown

Sections: Your score report will break down your performance by section.
Analysis: Use this to understand your strengths and weaknesses.

- If You Pass

Celebrate

Take a Moment: You've earned it! Celebrate your accomplishment.

Thank Supporters: Don't forget to thank those who helped you along the way.

Licensing Process

Application: Complete any remaining steps in your license application.

Fees: Pay any outstanding fees related to your license.

Issuance: Your license will be issued after all requirements and fees are met.

First Steps in Your Career

Brokerage: Decide where you want to hang your license. Research brokerages to find a good fit.

Networking: Start building your professional network.

Continuing Education: Look into courses or certifications that could benefit you.

- If You Fail

Don't Despair

It's Common: Many people don't pass on their first attempt.

Analyze: Use your score breakdown to understand where you went wrong.

Reapply

Waiting Period: Check if there's a mandatory waiting period before you can retake the exam.

Fees: You'll likely have to pay the exam fee again.

Study Again

Review: Go back to your study materials and focus on your weak areas.

Practice Exams: Take more practice exams to improve.

- Career Planning

Short-Term Goals

1. **First Sale**: Set a realistic timeframe for your first sale.
2. **Skill Development**: Identify key skills you need to develop.

Long-Term Goals

Specialization: Consider if you want to specialize in a certain type of real estate.

Scaling: Think about how you'll grow your business.

- Legal and Ethical Responsibilities

Code of Ethics: Familiarize yourself with the REALTOR® Code of Ethics.

State Laws: Make sure you understand all legal responsibilities in Illinois.

- Financial Planning

Budget: Real estate can be feast or famine. Plan your budget accordingly.

Taxes: Consult a tax advisor familiar with real estate income.

- Conclusion

The period after the Illinois Real Estate License Exam is a mix of relief, excitement, and planning. Whether you pass or fail, there are clear steps to take to either launch your career or prepare for another attempt. From understanding your results to setting career goals, each step is crucial in shaping your future in real estate. This chapter serves as a comprehensive guide for navigating this important phase, ensuring you're well-prepared for whatever comes next.

Career Development

Congratulations on passing the Illinois Real Estate License Exam and taking the first steps into your new career! The journey doesn't stop here; in fact, it's just beginning. This chapter aims to provide a comprehensive guide to career development in the Illinois real estate industry, covering everything from your first day on the job to long-term growth strategies.

- Your First Day as a Licensed Agent

Choosing a Brokerage

Research: Look into different brokerages and their cultures, commission structures, and training programs.
Interview: Meet with brokers to discuss your goals and see if their brokerage aligns with them.

Onboarding Process

Paperwork: Expect to fill out employment forms, tax documents, and possibly a contract.
Orientation: Many brokerages offer an orientation to familiarize you with their systems and procedures.

Your Workstation

Desk and Supplies: You'll likely be provided with a desk and basic office supplies.
Tech Setup: Make sure your computer, phone, and other tech are set up and ready to go.

- Building Your Brand

Personal Branding

Unique Value Proposition: What sets you apart from other agents?

Logo and Design: Consider creating a professional logo and design scheme for your marketing materials.

Online Presence

Website: A personal website can serve as a portfolio and lead generation tool.

Social Media: Platforms like LinkedIn, Instagram, and Facebook are excellent for networking and marketing.

Networking

Industry Events: Attend real estate events to meet other professionals.

Client Relationships: Always ask satisfied clients for referrals and testimonials.

- Skill Development

Sales Skills

Pitching: Learn how to effectively pitch your services to potential clients.

Closing: Master the art of closing a deal, from overcoming objections to signing contracts.

Technical Skills

MLS Systems: Become proficient in using Multiple Listing Service (MLS) systems.

Data Analysis: Learn how to interpret market data to better serve your clients.

Soft Skills

Communication: Effective communication is key in real estate.

Time Management: Learn how to manage your time to juggle various tasks and responsibilities.

- Financial Planning

Budgeting

Income and Expenses: Keep track of your income and expenses to understand your financial health.
Emergency Fund: It's wise to have an emergency fund for slow months.

Investments

Real Estate: Consider investing in real estate yourself.
Retirement: Don't forget long-term financial planning like retirement funds.

- Scaling Your Business

Hiring an Assistant

When to Hire: If administrative tasks are taking up too much time, it may be time to hire an assistant.
Virtual vs. In-Person: Weigh the pros and cons of a virtual assistant versus an in-person one.

Expanding Your Team

New Agents: As you grow, you may want to bring on new agents.
Specialists: Consider hiring specialists for areas like marketing or finance.

- Continuing Education and Certifications

State Requirements: Illinois requires ongoing education to renew your license.
Specializations: Certifications in areas like commercial real estate or property management can make you more marketable.

- Long-Term Career Paths

Brokerage Ownership: Some agents aspire to open their own brokerages.

Consulting: With enough experience, you could become a real estate consultant.

- Conclusion

Career development in real estate is a long-term commitment that requires planning, skill development, and adaptability. From your first day at the brokerage to the day you decide to scale your business or even start your own, each phase is crucial. This chapter has aimed to provide a roadmap for your career journey in the Illinois real estate market, equipping you with the knowledge and insights you need to succeed.

Conclusion

Wow, you did it! You've turned the last page, or perhaps scrolled to the end of this digital guide, "Illinois Real Estate License Exam: Best Test Prep Book to Help You Get Your License!" Give yourself a pat on the back; you've earned it. But let's be clear: finishing this book is not the end—it's just the beginning of your exciting journey into the Illinois real estate market.

Reflecting on Our Time Together

We've been through a lot, haven't we? From the nitty-gritty details of the Illinois real estate market to the complex laws and ethical considerations that govern it, we've covered it all. And let's not forget those mock exams and practice questions. They were tough but necessary. They were your training ground, designed to prepare you for the real deal: the Illinois Real Estate License Exam.

The Dynamic World of Real Estate

Real estate is not a static field; it's a living, breathing entity that evolves with time. Laws change, market trends shift, and technology advances at a breakneck pace. So, while this book has given you a solid foundation, your education shouldn't stop here. Keep learning. Attend seminars, read industry publications, and network with other professionals. The more you invest in your knowledge and skills, the higher your career will soar.

So, What's Next on the Agenda?

Are you ready for the Illinois Real Estate License Exam? Feeling a bit nervous? That's completely normal. But remember, you've got this. You've prepared, and now it's time to shine. For those of you who are already in the field, maybe it's time to take your career to the next level. Have you considered specializing in a particular type of real estate? Or perhaps you're ready to mentor newcomers to the industry. The sky's the limit!

A Heartfelt Thank You

I want to take a moment to express my gratitude. Thank you for trusting this book to guide you through the maze that is Illinois real estate. It's been an honor to be part of your journey. As you move forward, carry the lessons you've learned here close to your heart.

Final Words of Wisdom

As you step into the world of real estate, remember that your attitude will shape your journey. Be curious, be humble, and most importantly, be resilient. You're going to face challenges—that's a given. But it's how you overcome those challenges that will define your career.

So, here's to you and your future in Illinois real estate! May your journey be filled with success, and may your transactions always close smoothly.

Made in the USA
Monee, IL
08 November 2024

69637529R00144